Endorse

James Eade's vividly detailed memoir about his struggles to maintain his sobriety in comfort provides insights, cautions, and hope to the millions of recovering addicts embarking on their own journeys towards fulfilling, sober lives.

Mel Thrash, M.D.

James clearly explains his spiritual path and "what works for him" in recovery. This positive, helpful, and personal book will encourage others in doing the same. The chapters in *Freedom* are human, believable, and original. His gifted writing doesn't just talk about, but conveys the sense of freedom the title expresses. Enthusiastic thumbs up.

An AA Member

When a person in recovery takes the time to explain his path out of addiction, it's a gift to those of us who want to understand.

D'Anne Burwell
Author, *Saving Jake: When Addiction Hits Home*

A story of recovery and about recovery. A book of hope, and hopeful possibilities for each and every addict.

Yudhisthira Doug Andrews
Co-leader, Yoga and the 12 Steps

The central, positive message full of hope in James Eade's book, *Freedom: Your Path to Recovery* needs to reach all who experience addiction and all medical and mental health professionals who work with them. That message: there are different communities, methods, and practices available to meet the recovery needs of different people. Jim generously, openly, and clearly tells his story, from the roots of his life-threatening addiction to finding his path to recovery. Along the way, he participates in different approaches to addiction, learning that "The path to finding freedom is up to the individual." Jim describes in easy-to-understand ways how his journey helped him to reconcile contemporary life with ancient wisdom, and spiritual sensibilities with scientific thinking. Jim's path also uncovered that mercy and forgiveness (toward self and others) can lead to peace and calm, a valuable lesson for all of us trying to cope with life's successes and failures, hopes and disappointments, frustrations and joys.

Mary Coakley-Welch, Ph.D.
Licensed Psychologist, Neuropsychologist

Eade has written an important book on coping with addiction. He writes with precision, passion, and panache. Eade is a good read.

Tim Redman, Ph.D.
Professor Emeritus of Literary Studies, The University of Texas at Dallas

FREEDOM

YOUR PATH TO RECOVERY

JAMES EADE

HIGHERLIFE
PUBLISHING & MARKETING

Freedom

© 2023 by Jim Eade. All rights reserved.

HigherLife Development Services, Inc.

P.O. Box 623307

Oviedo, FL 32762

(407) 563-4806

www.ahigherlife.com

ISBN: 978-1-958211-32-8 (paperback)

978-1-958211-33-5 (ebook)

Library of Congress Control Number: 2022950911

Printed in the United States of America.

10 9 8 7 6 5 4 3 2 1

DEDICATION

To my wife, Sheri Anderson. Addiction is a family affair.
I dedicate this to her as part of my amends for
the pain and suffering that I caused in our marriage.

CONTENTS

PREFACE

DID YOU EXPECT A preface?

That's a mistake.

Having expectations is a mistake, according to Alcoholics Anonymous (AA). Expectations set you up for resentments, and resentments will take you out. However, when you turn your steering wheel, you expect your car to turn in the same direction, right? Of course, you do. But holding two apparently contradictory thoughts in your head at once is a sign of recovery.

Welcome to my world.

When you learn to comfortably hold two contradictory thoughts in your mind and accept that they are both true, you will find that addiction is a delusion. You will learn that you are looking at things through a veil of delusion. Then the realization might sink in that after you strip off one veil, there is yet another and another.

Do not be discouraged! This is when it becomes work. A life's work.

But that's when the fun begins!

Life is but a game. There are no winners or losers in the game of life. No one is keeping score.

What matters is how you play the game. When addicts accept this, they experience peace of mind that helps them to recover and stay in recovery.

This is a story of how I found my way and how I play the game today.

INTRODUCTION

THIS IS NOT AN Alcoholics Anonymous-bashing book. For a very long time AA has done a wonderful job helping alcoholics abstain from alcohol. It has also done something that is nearly impossible—it is not out to profit from anyone's misery. It is just there to help.

Yet, I was not a good fit for AA. If I am honest about what didn't work for me, it will be difficult to avoid seeming judgmental. This is a delicate dance, and I wish to tell those who do not find what they need in AA to continue their search. It is not for everyone.

It is also important for medical professionals, therapists, clergy, and others seeking to help alcoholics recover to know that AA is not the only recovery program available. There are theistic, monistic, pantheistic, and non-theistic programs out there. Encourage your clients to keep searching for the one that fits them best. There is no reason to simultaneously not attend more than one. Just don't give up the search.

It was my experience that AA scratched the surface of what I needed to continue walking the path of recovery. AA was established by a small group of male White Anglo-Saxon Protestants (WASPs) in the early to mid-twentieth century. If you are comfortable with that mindset, AA might be exactly what you need. It has tried to change with the times, but it hasn't learned to let go of what no longer serves.

AA also tends to assign blame to those that have difficulty accepting its program of recovery.

At every meeting I attended, someone would read a portion of the book *Alcoholics Anonymous* titled "How It Works." They would claim that those unable to follow this simple program were usually unable to be honest with themselves.

I thought that this was malarkey.

Who is capable of being rigorously honest with themselves?

Who sets the standards?

What metrics are used?

I never met anyone capable of being completely honest with themselves. Why did they think that was the issue?

There were many reasons AA doesn't work for everyone. But the groups I knew, full of intelligent people, did not want to accept this. Their founders didn't want to accept this. I believe this continues holding the organization back from adapting to the times.

They do have a well-established change mechanism, although it is cumbersome and slow to put into action. The difficulty is that it begins with raising an issue at the group level. It bubbles up from there. Good luck raising a change item at the group level! You will need more patience than I had. And a thicker skin.

I was never able to achieve even a moderate level of success. I was told that I was arrogant. I was told that I was "terminally unique" and was met with other wonderful versions of AA smack talk. I guess I was the problem. I gave up trying to change AA after five-and-a-half years. But I found different programs that were a better fit for me. They were called Refuge Recovery and Recovery Dharma.

The point is not that one is good and the other bad. The point is to keep trying until you find a program that works for you. AA is not a good fit for all. Refuge Recovery is not a good fit for all. We all need to try to stop thinking in terms of what is good or bad, and focus on what works for each individual addict.

Addiction comes in all shapes and sizes. The alcoholic is just an addict like any other. Addiction leads to unnecessary pain and suffering. Freedom is achieved not by focusing on the addiction itself but by focusing on the underlying causes of the addiction. With awareness comes power. Every individual has the power and potential to free themselves of addiction. The first step is to regain hope. Ideally, you will eventually find enough hope to share with others. That's how it works. You share your hope with those within your sphere of influence, and they share their hope with those within theirs.

It must start somewhere.

Why not with you?

CHAPTER ONE

RECOVERY

WE ARE OFTEN TOLD to begin at the beginning. If we have the power of choice, we can begin wherever we like.

I will begin in the middle.

Addiction robs us of the power of choice. It is a merciless tyrant that causes pain and suffering for the addict—and the addict's loved ones.

Recovery is not the endgame. But we cannot get where we want to go without understanding what recovery means, and why it is so important to achieve. Recovering the power of choice returns the addict the power to renounce the substances or behaviors that compelled them while in the throes of addiction.

Recovery is not merely abstinence. Abstinence can be achieved by many means, including the addict's own willpower. Abstinence may not be sustainable unless recovery has begun. There is no special spiritual quality to abstinence, but there is to recovery. Programs that define themselves as abstinence-based cause my "spider sense" to tingle. Abstinence can be a byproduct of renunciation, and renunciation is the key to recovery. Abstinence alone achieves little. The phrase "white knuckling it" is often used to describe a person who is merely abstaining from the substance or behavior they had become addicted to. It is a strain to maintain. It is inherently fragile and can crack at any time. It isn't until the spiritual quality of renunciation is achieved that any addict will find peace and serenity. Misery remains until renunciation frees the addict from the slavery of compulsion.

Just as renunciation is not abstinence, spirituality is not religion. If you achieve the spiritual quality of renunciation, it matters little whether you do so in a church, temple, synagogue, mosque, or other house of worship. It can also be achieved outside of such places. The main point is that you are unlikely to do it alone. A sense of community seems to be one of the key factors in achieving recovery.

If you do so within a religious community, you are blessed. The community has already been established and you will find that you belong. If not, you will need to find a community or Sangha another way. Fortunately, there are programs that addicts have developed that are not based on any religious practice, but on a type of spirituality that was freely given to us. We simply need to recover it.

Addicts typically live in a world of delusion.

Addicts typically live in a world of delusion. We see the world through a veil of delusion and can justify our harmful behavior despite all evidence to the contrary. Recovering this spiritual sense returns to us the power of choice. We can learn to choose wisely—discerning the difference between delusion and reality. Recovery allows us to remove the first veil of delusion, but it doesn't mean we are done. For every veil we remove, we may find another one underneath.

Is recovery an endless and ultimately fruitless journey? Of course not.

Whenever we remove a veil of delusion, we make progress. And it is progress, not perfection, that we should hang our hats on. Although we see more clearly each time we remove a veil, we must not allow ourselves to fall into the trap of thinking we are seeing all that there is to see.

We are not superior.

We need to practice humility.

We need to remind ourselves that however much we know, we only know a little. There is always more to be learned. Quite often, we do not know what we need to hear until we hear it. Even then, it does us no good unless we are mindfully listening. Mindful listening is one of the tools we can learn to use on our road to recovery.

When you find a community that works for you, you will encounter other tools people have used to help them on their road to recovery. I have found that what works for them does not always work for me, and what works for me does not always work for them. You are the only one who can possibly know what works for you.

But how will you know? In the beginning, your judgment will be clouded. If your experience is anything like mine, it will improve over time. You will develop an inner resonance that informs you when you are on the right track. Only you will have access to that inner resonance. As you develop it, your confidence will grow. You will not need the approval of others to know that you have chosen wisely. You will learn to not allow praise to go to your head, or criticism to go to your heart.

Things will begin to become intuitively obvious that were previously beyond your knowledge. Fear and shame will no longer be the source of misery. You will see them for what they are—feelings and nothing more. Emotions do not last. They come and go. They are impermanent. You do not have to react to them or be ruled by them. You can choose to feel them without giving into them. They will no longer rule your life.

You will recover your sense of worth. You will recover the intuitive wisdom that was freely given to us all. You will know right action from wrong. You will not have to be told these things or be instructed about them. You will know them by looking within. That is where the answers have always been. We were just disconnected from ourselves.

These answers are not ours alone. They are within all beings who allow themselves to be connected. My disease was one of disconnection. I thought isolation was my refuge, but it was my trap. Connecting to others is a key and connecting to forces beyond our control is the ultimate answer.

I thought people were the problem.

I thought that by isolating myself from them I would be fine.

I only found pain and misery in my isolation.

I self-medicated to mask the pain and suffering.

By connecting to people and forces beyond my control, I was able to recover a sense of belonging, of self-worth. I was able to find peace and serenity.

Of course, this was not sustainable for me all day, every day. I would still become anxious or agitated at some point during the day. I was able to develop spiritual rituals that would return me to a place of connectedness where I could recover in peace and serenity. If I performed these rituals every morning, I could begin my day feeling empowered, healthy, and spiritually fit. Even so, at some point in the day, I would inevitably feel anxious or agitated all over again. If I had begun my day by getting connected, I knew that I could recover my sense of peace and serenity. The technique or tool I would use was deep breathing. You will find what works for you. Impermanence, the simple fact that nothing lasts forever, is reality. You will never stay anxious or at peace unless you achieve enlightenment.

Enlightenment may be the ultimate goal, but freedom from the pain and suffering of addiction comes first.

You can recover your sense of self-worth, well-being, and ease. This is the promise that one recovering addict makes to another. You must make it your highest priority. It cannot be an afterthought or postponed to a future date. It must be a commitment.

Fortunately, you do not have to do it forever. That would be an enormous burden, too heavy to carry. You just must do it every day, one day at a time. Even though it may never get easy, it does get easier.

All beings have the power and potential to recover from addiction. With the support of your community, people who are seeking, finding, or walking their own spiritual path, you will recover.

Your entire way of thinking and being will change. You will find peace and serenity. I promise. I can only tell you what happened to me. Twelve-step programs often cite Carl Jung as saying that he never saw an addict (alcoholic) recover unless it involved a spiritual transformation. That's what happened to me. I always identified as a humanist or a rationalist. I had confused spirituality with religion. That was one of my many delusions.

One's spiritual path may be religious, or it may not. Identifying as religious does not mean that you have found, let alone walked, your spiritual path. I have met spiritual people who are religious, and I have met religious people who are not spiritual. There is no need to join a religion, or cult, to find and walk your spiritual path. Just find your community or Sangha.

I found it discouraging to share my spiritual awakening with members of the twelve-step community. They could not relate to it or accept it as a reality. So, I devised a story that they found more acceptable for them. I will share my real spiritual awakening later, but for now, I will tell you what I told them.

It was my experience that addicts (alcoholics) could come from anywhere. It didn't matter what country they were from, or what language they spoke. We would all find ourselves in a similar place. In the story I told, my way forward was blocked by a massive, unscalable oak. The only way forward was to walk around it on one side or the other.

One side was brilliantly lit. The light was almost blinding. The way seemed blocked by an ever-ascending staircase. The first step seemed too tall to get past. My most outstretched fingertip could merely touch the top of the step. There was no way that I could get a grip and hoist myself up onto it.

The other way was darker and easier on the eyes. It appeared to be descending very slowly. Naturally, I chose the easier softer way. The gradual descent continued, and I congratulated myself on the wisdom of my choice. Only fools would have chosen the other path, which was obviously much more difficult, I told myself.

The descent became steeper very soon after this thought, and it became suddenly damp. The dampness and angle of descent increased with every step. I almost lost my balance a few times, and I began to worry. I completely lost my balance with one step and fell, flailing my arms uselessly.

I started to slide down the slope, failing to stop myself. A moment of panic was replaced by a feeling of exhilaration. Sometimes falling feels like flying!

I was ecstatic! I thought I had stumbled upon the answer to all of life's problems.

The rate of descent increased, and a branch whipped across my face, stinging it sharply. I then glanced against a rock that banged and scraped my shoulder painfully. The fun was over. Another rock was followed by another branch, and I desperately wanted to stop my fall.

No matter how hard I tried, I could not secure a handhold on anything. My ecstasy was long forgotten. I knew that my descent would only be broken when I reached the bottom. I fell until I had given up all hope of stopping myself.

I then was staring at the abyss. I heard the screams of others who had fallen over the edge, and I was soon to be next. With one final desperate stab of my hand, I caught onto something strong enough to stop me. None too soon, I might add, because my legs were dangling over the abyss.

I lay there panting before I pulled myself up to solid, though mushy, ground. I looked up at the long upward climb back and gave in to despair. There was just no way that I could make my way back to the top of that steep, slimy slope.

Then I experienced my spiritual awakening. I drew strength from a source I had no way of naming. I knew that the abyss was still waiting for me, and I had no intention of ending up there. My only choice was to climb. Even if every step took all my courage and strength to climb, I had no choice but to take each and every difficult step back to where I started. I then began my ascent from what people call my spiritual bottom, back to what I call my spiritual bankruptcy.

I gave no thought to what I would do then.

It was all I could do to climb and hope that I could get back to where I had already been.

I climbed, and I climbed. I grew exhausted and discouraged. Every time I considered giving up, something happened to keep me going. My mind was so exhausted that it happened all in a fog. Certainly, I must have dreamed the next parts.

Whenever I was too dejected to go on, something or someone came to my aid. I would reach my hand out blindly and there would be another hand to take it. It gave me the strength to carry on. Sometimes it felt as though I was getting a swift kick in my backside to spur me on to an even greater effort. I became convinced that I was not alone.

Finally, after what seemed like a lifetime of struggle, I pulled myself back to the place I once stood so sure of myself and my destiny. After regaining enough strength to stand again, I found myself looking at that same massive, unscalable oak. I had the same two choices to go around it.

> **Whenever I was too dejected to go on, something or someone came to my aid.**

This time, fortunately, I was just a bit wiser. I knew where that gently sloping descent ended. I decided not to take that path again. I looked again carefully at the nearly blinding lighted path that I had rejected before. How was I going to take that first step?

Inspiration flooded into my mind. A ray of hope followed it. I could not scale the oak, but I could run up it just enough to launch myself at the top of the step and maybe grab onto it! I did my best to calculate the speed and trajectory I would need and became determined to try. My first couple of attempts failed, but on my third try I got an arm up over it and held on.

I was able to get my other arm over the side and hang on with my elbows providing a firm resting place. After a couple of swings and misses, I was able to swing one leg up and over. I was then free to swing my entire body over the step! Fortunately, it was a short drop from there. Before I could spend too much time congratulating myself, I realized that there was another step, just as foreboding, blocking my path once again.

I would end the story there, and people were receptive and enthusiastic in response. I knew that my truth was not understood, but people wanted and needed to hear the story.

I have found that a spiritual path is sometimes a lonely one. On my road to recovery, I learned the lesson that it was more important for me to understand, rather than to be understood.

It was only later, when I found the spiritual path I was meant to walk, that I learned another important lesson. Even if you are all by yourself, you are never truly alone. Once connected, always connected. That realization has served me well over the years. I no longer see people as the problem but as part of the solution.

Isolation was my downfall.

Community was my refuge.

I was able to find my path and walk it. I did so with my head held high looking people in the eye. I was a long way away from the person who was desperate to avoid human contact. I was able to see the pain and suffering of others and find my role in easing it. Service to others became a gift I gave to myself. I was well on the road to recovery.

CHAPTER TWO

TRAUMA

I T DOESN'T SEEM TO matter what your addiction is. Whether it is hard drugs, video games, the need to control others, or alcohol and nicotine, as it was in my case, recovery seems to be "recovery" in all instances. It is often just a question of finding your spiritual path and walking it. It can also be done purely rationally, as Krishna is said to have told Arjuna in the *Bhagavad Gita*. Krishna also warns that it will be more difficult, but that it can be done.

The other common factor for addicts seems to be trauma. When we search for the cause of our addiction, we tend to find trauma of some kind at the root. Trauma causes us to develop defense mechanisms, which can be as deep as denial, or as superficial as fake acceptance.

It doesn't seem to matter what kind of trauma it is. It serves no purpose to compare the types of traumas or rank them from valid to invalid. The perception of trauma is all that truly matters—the individual's perception and the lengths they go to protect themselves from it—in recovery.

Many of us have buried the trauma under layers of denial. It can be difficult even to recover the memories if they have been buried deep enough. Talk therapy can be useful in unearthing the trauma of the past. Sometimes the mere act of bringing the trauma into consciousness from the subconscious can be enough to allow the healing process to begin.

If addiction has become part of your coping strategy, however, talk therapy may be necessary but insufficient. Getting into recovery is also essential. Often therapists are ill-equipped to help with this. Many will refer you to a twelve-step type of program because that is all that they know. What if those programs do not meet your needs?

It is important for therapists to learn about other types of recovery programs as potential resources to meet their clients' needs. They will be in a good position to give advice if they know about available options.

This is where the success of the twelve-step programs becomes a double-edged sword. Although their retention rate is quite low, they have had undoubted success with millions of people. They have also earned the trust of the public. They are not scams. They are not money-making operations. They are non-profit organizations that exist to help those in need.

This is truly commendable, and they should be lauded for the service that they provide. One size does not fit all, however. The AA program I was referred to was operating under a mindset that was formed in the mid-20th century and created by White Anglo-Saxon Protestants (WASPs).

I was not a WASP.

I had a 21st-century mindset.

This caused me a great deal of angst, especially when I was told that the program was not the problem. That I was.

They claimed that I lacked humility and was arrogant. Why couldn't I simply accept the wisdom of the program? I was told that if I did not, I would not remain sober.

I did not know which way to turn. That is why I am sharing my experience with others. Please, stay true to yourself. Find what works for you. There are other options out there.

Later, I will write more about the alternatives I found and why they were a better fit for me during my recovery. For the moment, let's return to the subject of trauma. Trauma leads to fear and shame. These are two of the lowest vibrations in the universe. I have never made a wise decision operating out of either fear or shame.

When we experience trauma, we want to escape the feelings of fear and shame. Some of us choose to self-medicate and cover up these feelings. We wish to escape the pain and suffering by numbing ourselves to them. I certainly did that myself.

We can also turn to other types of addictive substances and behavior to free ourselves from pain and suffering. We can try to get high to escape the feelings of fear and shame. This was my initial coping mechanism.

I wanted to get higher than high.

I wanted to feel ecstatic.

Chasing after the feeling of ecstasy was initially rewarding. I entered a world of sex, drugs, and rock 'n' roll. I will not pretend that I did not have ecstatic experiences. I certainly did.

> **When we experience trauma, we want to escape the feelings of fear and shame.**

I also found that these experiences were not sustainable. The highs were followed by lows. The cost of the lows began to exceed the benefits of the highs. In my college days we would often start the day by sharing a joint. We called this "getting right." In truth, we were all probably dehydrated from the previous night's drinking, and a tall glass of water would have helped us more. The fix was a trap. We simply did not know any better.

Once you begin to try to fix yourself you are heading down the road to addiction. It takes more and more of whatever you are using to fix yourself to produce the same results. You will find that you need the fix. You are no longer choosing it. When you are in the throes, you feel compelled to indulge yourself with whatever substances or behaviors you had previously chosen to escape pain and suffering.

You have lost the power of choice.

But you can regain this power.

All beings have the potential to do so. We rarely can do it

alone. Community and communication are keys to recovering the power of choice that was once freely given to us. Isolation is often the addict's choice, however, and this inevitably leads only to more pain and suffering.

It is necessary to identify the cause of your trauma, but that only gets you to square one. You must also learn to cope with the fear and shame associated with this trauma. We are not taught healthy coping skills. In fact, what we are taught is to deny the trauma. No one wants to talk about it!

We sometimes seek therapy to find a safe place to talk about these things, which are not acceptable to speak about in polite society. The other place we have, but are rarely told about, is the community of like-minded fellow sufferers. These communities are often treated as social lepers themselves. To seek one of them out is to admit that you have a problem. In a society based on self-sufficiency, you will be met with derision and the certainty that there is something wrong with you.

There is nothing wrong with you.

You are not broken.

You do not need a fix or to be fixed.

All beings have the power and potential to free themselves from the pain and suffering caused by addiction. This means you have that power too.

Do not give in to despair. Addicts know the feeling of incomprehensible demoralization and hopelessness. Many of us have recovered from them. The alternative to recovery is dire indeed. Most of us have witnessed the demise of those who never found recovery. It is not a pretty thing to see.

It will require courage and determination, qualities you may think you lack. However, with the support of a community around you, you will find that those qualities are within you. They need to be encouraged and supported, but they were always there. Isolation almost cost me my life, but I was certain at the time that it was what was best for me.

Once your mind has been cleared of the delusions of addiction, your decision-making will improve. Your thinking will no longer be trapped in the four corners of delusion. Even with clearer thinking you are not yet free from the delusions your ego will try to convince you represent reality. Detachment from the ego is a huge step towards recovery. This will take time and effort, but it can be done. Whatever trauma you have experienced, whatever defense mechanisms you have put in place to make you feel safe, however low you have gone, there is hope.

Prior to investigating my own trauma, I had to develop a mindset based on understanding, forgiveness, and compassion. I came to realize that just as the past forms us, it can inform us if we approach it from a place of generosity and healing. It was important for me to realize that my parents had their own sufferings and their own defense mechanisms and were doing the best they could.

Rather than blame them for any trauma I had experienced, it was important for me to understand

- what the trauma was,
- how it manifested itself in continued suffering,
- and how I could come to accept it and free myself from its tyranny.

It most clearly manifested itself in my childhood through reoccurring nightmares. I don't know when it began, but probably around six years old, if not earlier. I remember this for a rather silly reason.

My favorite baseball player was Mickey Mantle. His number was seven. I can vividly recall thinking, in that magical childlike way, that when I turned seven the nightmares would stop. They did not.

I can recall trying as hard as I could to not fall asleep, but I always did. As soon as the nightmare would start, I could usually identify which one it would be. There were variations, of course, and the exception to this rule would be those that started off as happy ones. They would fool me for a while, but they would inevitably turn dark, and take on terror-inducing tones.

There were the old standbys where I would be running in place, yet unable to move. There was one, when Mighty Joe Young, from the movie of the same name, would be chasing me. He would always catch me, of course, but instead of what you might expect, he would tickle me. Obviously, someone bigger and stronger than myself had subjected me to tortuous tickling at some point in my childhood.

Most often, the nightmares would feature either a nice woman turning into a witch or one that was incredibly large and trying to force me to do something I desperately did not want to do. I always lost these power struggles and woke up in a state of panic. This happened every night. I would have a nightmare of some kind. I have included a photo of myself a little older, but still suffering from those recurring nightmares.

These nighttime traumas caused anxiety. I would often only feel safe when I was alone. Of course, when you go to school, you are rarely allowed to be alone, so school became a source of acute anxiety for me. I determined that since I had to go to school, and I hated being in school, the only recourse was for me to make school hate me.

A couple of teachers seemed to understand and were able to reach me. The rest would do things like put my desk in a back corner, send me to the principal, or otherwise treat me as an outcast. I came to identify as an outcast. This is an addict in waiting.

An early principal—probably sick of seeing me—would send me to the school library. This was exactly what I needed. I could be alone and read books that interested me. I was always able to get Bs in school because there were always books at my home that interested me. I became a ferocious reader. No one in my classes would be reading what I was reading, and that reinforced my alienation and sense of estrangement.

I was also very good at math. When one teacher—she knew I had been absent when the material had been introduced in the class—gave a pop quiz, I managed to ace it. I will never forget the look on her face when she handed the paper back to me with an A on it. She thought she had trapped me, and she was furious that I had escaped the trap!

This was a childhood of anxiety, confrontation, and defiance. I was only happy when I was alone or when my younger brother and I were making up stories together, or when I was playing a game. Games had rules, and I could learn the rules, and everyone had to play by the same ones. This seemed fair and just. Much as life seemed unfair and unjust.

This experience was largely unchanged until the 5th grade. I read *The Teachings of Don Juan* by Carlos Castaneda. Everything changed. No one else in my class was reading Castaneda, so there was no one for me to talk to about it.

But I was used to that.

I learned the secret to controlling my dreams. Don Juan taught that you could control your dreams by intentionally looking at your hand. This seemed to be a ridiculously simple solution, but I was desperate enough to try anything. It worked!

That night I had the regular nightmare where Frankenstein's Monster was lumbering towards me. I knew that if I tried to run, I would be stuck in place. How many times had I had that same nightmare? This time it was different.

I looked at the palm of my hand.

I now had a feeling of control over what happened next.

When I looked again at the Monster, it was smiling at me.

That began the end of my recurring nightmares.

My life could be perfect now, right? No. I had developed all those defense mechanisms to manage my constant state of anxiety, and I was still enslaved by them. I would behave in ways that were harmful to myself and to others. I had lost the power of choice.

The pattern of anxiety, confrontation, and defiance still ruled my waking life even after the nightmares ceased to rule my sleep. It ruled my life for decades until I began to recover from my addictions and my lifelong patterns of behavior. In recovery, I learned to discard the old defense mechanisms, which no longer served, and replace them with tools that ultimately allowed me to regain the power of choice.

I could choose to behave in different ways than I had in the past.

It wasn't overnight.

It wasn't easy.

But I did it.

I am still not perfect at making the right choice and I doubt that I ever will be. It is not perfection that is the goal. It is progress. Sometimes this progress can only be perceived over time. You look back at your behavior in the past and realize that you are no longer behaving that way anymore.

This realization produced something akin to joy. The feeling of freedom is a joyous one. The path to finding this freedom is up to the individual.

We must find it for ourselves. You may find it in a community. You may find it in any number of ways. Once you find it you must walk it. Only you will truly know whether the path you have found is the path you must follow. Even if a million people have found their freedom by walking a particular path, that does not mean their path is the path for you.

Walking someone else's path will not free you from pain and suffering. Walking your own, with your head held high and looking people in the eye, just might. Most of us put our feet wrong from time to time. That is when a community can be of its greatest service. The support of a community can set you back on your path, even if they are not walking it with you.

I hope you will find a community of people seeking their path.

Seekers will help you to find.

Seeking will not guarantee that you will find, but only seekers find.

Seek.

CHAPTER THREE

COMMUNITY AND COMMUNICATION

FINDING A COMMUNITY MAY be one of the most essential ingredients to recovery. This was a difficult lesson for me to learn. For much of my life, I lived by the old Groucho Marx joke: "I refuse to join any club that would have me for a member."

Although Groucho was being funny, humor often masks other underlying feelings. In my case, it was a lack of self-worth. If you were foolish enough to want me as part of your club, well, that told me all I needed to know about you. This is the addict's constant battle. Feelings of grandiosity coupled with feelings of worthlessness. An uneasy truce is the unsatisfying best outcome.

When I was feeling good about myself, I thought I was self-sufficient. Our society encourages that sort of thought. Growing up on John Wayne movies only drives that message deeper. It was a lie I told myself. I never cut my own hair, and I never filled my own cavities but somehow, I thought that I could be a self-made man.

When I was feeling low, I thought I was a failure at everything. My successes meant nothing; my failures meant everything. My own perspective was almost always off-target. I could only get an objective measure of myself through the eyes of others who knew me well. My actions, however, prevented anyone from knowing me well enough to give me accurate feedback.

My behavior reinforced my sense of alienation and estrangement. Isolation was what I sought, and isolation only increased my suffering. Like it or not—and I didn't like it—I had to find a community.

What does community mean? Language can be ambiguous. We often think we are talking about the same thing when we use the same words. However, we are often talking past ourselves, and end up disappointed when a misunderstanding arises. I have found it critical for me to be clear about the definition of terms. Only then will I have a chance to avoid miscommunication.

I learned about what community means to me when I learned about Sangha. What does Sangha mean? This is the definition from the Recovery Dharma website:

> Sangha is the third of the Three Jewels: loosely translated, it means "community." It's where Buddha and Dharma find their expression, where we're supported in putting those principles into action. It's a community of friends practicing the dharma together in order to develop our own awareness and maintain it. The traditional definition of sangha originally described monastic communities of ordained monks and nuns, but in many Buddhist traditions it has evolved to include the wider spiritual community. For us, our sangha is our community of both dharma practice and recovery.[1]

This is a Buddhist concept, but one that fits me. I was looking for a spiritual community based on the common suffering of addiction. Addicts often speak the same language. There is less of a need to define one's terms with fellow addicts, and I also knew that my recovery from addiction was going to involve the awakening of my spirit.

Addicts can use a thousand words with non-addicts and not achieve true communication.

Addicts can use less than a dozen words with fellow addicts and find them nodding their heads in understanding.

---

1   *Recovery Dharma*, p. 52, https://recoverydharma.org/book/.

Take the word "craving" as an example. Most people believe they understand what this word means. This leads to miscommunication and misunderstanding because addicts and non-addicts do not think of the word in the same way. The difference involves frequency and intensity. Everyone has experienced a craving of some kind. If they are infrequent enough, or low enough in intensity, we can develop the delusion of control. This can lead people to think that addicts simply lack self-control, but that is not the case.

Addiction is a subtle process. It is not well understood by non-addicts. The addict does not face cravings that are like the cravings of the non-addict. They are not infrequent. They are very intense. I learned this with my struggle to get free from my addiction to cigarettes.

When I was on writing deadlines I would write for a while, and then stop to read what I had written. I slowly developed the habit of smoking a cigarette while reading. This used to be an occasional thing I did, but it gradually became consistent. I don't remember why I started. Perhaps I was under the delusion that it would help me concentrate, or perhaps it was because it temporarily eased my deadline anxiety, but it certainly snuck up on me.

When I tried to quit, I was surprised to find that it was not going to be as easy as I expected. I would get a craving, and I would resist it. This would happen repeatedly. I would resist the urge hundreds of times, but, if I gave in just once, I would be back to my old way of behaving.

The frequency of the cravings wore me down. If they would only happen now and then, it would be one thing. But they resurfaced almost as soon as I had swatted them away. This frequency says nothing about the intensity. That is another variable, but one just as difficult to manage.

Sometimes, the intensity of the craving an addict experiences is literally gut-wrenching. If this has never happened to you, do not be so quick to judge those of us who have. The judgment of others leads to shame. Shame spirals into self-loathing for many addicts and it does nothing but disempower them from confronting their addictions.

Judging words will sound harsh to addicts. People will think they are being too sensitive, but the simple fact is that there is a lack of understanding at play. People assume they know what the addict is going through when they do not. The addict will only find understanding in a community of fellow sufferers.

This community will understand. Communication is then possible. The community can help individuals find the tools that are helpful in recovery. They are less apt to be judgmental or give useless advice. "Just stop" or "Just say no" do not amount to helpful words for an addict to hear. Often, they come attached with an air of superiority which is off-putting at best.

Therefore, finding a community that works for you is of the utmost importance in recovery. It isn't important whether it works for others. It must work for you. If others try to convince you that their community is the only community that works, do not believe them. I have found multiple communities that work for many, many people. The trick is to find one that works for you. You are the only person capable of making that determination.

> **Finding a community that works for you is of the utmost importance in recovery.**

Medical professionals and therapists are often uninformed about the options available to you. This is when the work falls to you. You must be your own advocate. However, do not fall into a trap of looking for a community that allows you to make excuses for your behavior. Your behavior must change. It is the only hope you have.

The communities that accept you as you are will feel different from the ones that don't. Their absence of judging and advice-giving will feel refreshing. They have been where you are. If it is the right community for you, they will also show you tough love when you need it. They will not come from a place of superiority if they are doing things the right way. They will simply know that addicts are incredibly creative when making excuses for their own behavior. The most common excuse-making involves blaming others.

Addicts must learn to take responsibility for their own actions. A community will hold you accountable for your own actions. They will be able to communicate this to you in a way that feels supportive rather than demeaning. Remember, they have been where you are.

No community will be a perfect fit for you. You will encounter people that simply rub you the wrong way. Patience is a key tool to practice. This also did not come easily for me. I would often joke that "immediate gratification is not fast enough for me!" I was only half joking. I needed to learn to sit and reflect on things that got me agitated or caused me anxiety.

I was taught tools that helped me do this. Deep breathing became my go-to when I felt uneasy. This worked for me, but the main thing to remember is to find what works for you. After practicing one of the deep breathing tools long enough and consistently enough, I became proficient at it. One simple deep breath was enough to restore me to a sense of calmness. I never made good decisions when anxious or aggravated. I made much better decisions when I was calm. My behavior changed, and my life got easier.

There are many tools for you to choose from. You will find those that work best for you. I had to be open to trying them though. My tendency was to be dismissive. This is what addicts call contempt prior to investigation. The more willing I became to try new things, despite my self-assured skepticism, the more tools I found that worked for me.

I found that the body can calm the mind, just as the mind can calm the body. The key for me was awareness. I had to first become aware that I was anxious or agitated. I also had to have prepared my go-to tool beforehand. There is no sense in trying to make one up on the fly. That would rarely work for me.

After becoming aware of my state of mind at any moment in

time, it was possible for me to employ a tool that I had already become proficient at to change my behavior. Deep breathing would return me to a state of mindfulness. It helped me see that whatever I was anxious or agitated about was no big deal.

The negative feelings would slip away, and I could behave in a manner that produced better outcomes. I was no longer trapped in the cycle of a feeling producing a reaction that led to suboptimal behavior. I would feel that the power of choice had been returned to me. I would feel free.

This freedom, realizing that I had the power to choose, would produce in me a feeling of joy. This joy was a higher high than I had ever experienced by ingesting foreign substances. I had to learn not to cling to it. I had to learn not to chase it. I had to learn to be grateful for it.

This was a gift I could give to myself at any time, but it would be, like everything else, impermanent. I could experience the feeling of joy without needing to hold on to it. I could experience it and let it go. Only at this point did I feel as though I was making real progress in my recovery.

I found a way to communicate this experience to other sufferers. At least those of a certain age—like those that remembered record players! I would say that my brain had a well-worn groove in it. A stimulus would register at the base of my brain and travel the groove until it resulted in a behavior. Flight, fight, or freeze sorts of behaviors. I had no conscious role in choosing the behavior.

The communities I got involved in taught me the tools that allowed me to pause this process before it ran to completion. Though I could not stop the stimulus, I could become aware of it before the behavior was triggered. I was not always successful, but the more I worked on it the more successful I became.

After becoming aware of the stimulus, I could mentally pick the needle up from the old grove and move it to a new one. At first, it sounded scratchy and uncomfortable. But over time, it became smoother and smoother. The music it played sounded sweeter and sweeter. I could choose how to behave rather than have my behavior dictated to me. This freedom of choice was empowering.

When I was able to communicate this process to a fellow sufferer, they could understand it. It gave them hope. This community and communication would ease the pain and suffering that addiction causes. I could feel as though I was a part of something greater than myself.

I knew that this power of choice was freely given to me. It is freely given to all beings.

The confidence that all beings had the power and potential to free themselves from the pain and suffering of addiction grew until I manifested it in all aspects of my daily life.

Though I was still far from perfect, my progress was undeniable. I no longer found myself condemned to suffer from a sense of worthlessness. The joy I experienced in seeing others make progress was proof enough for me that there was a reason to get up out of bed each day. If I could help just one person experience what I had experienced it would be worthwhile. If I could do that, why wouldn't I?

The sense of community was a gift. The ability to communicate without elaborate explanations or excessive translations was a gift. I learned to appreciate these gifts and to be grateful for them.

Do not give into despair when so many people fail to understand you or judge you harshly. There exist communities where you will find understanding and support. It is up to you to find one that works for you.

I was only told about AA. That was not the best fit for me, but I did not know that other communities existed! I will not pretend that I have found them all. I can state with confidence that if you are willing to seek them out, the chances of you finding one that works for you are in your favor.

CHAPTER FOUR

WHAT HAPPENED

THIS ISN'T WHAT I tell people happened.

This is what happened.

I discovered that people just didn't seem to accept what really happened to me, so I made up a story that sounded close enough but was more or less relatable than what really happened. Having to do this reinforced my sense of alienation and estrangement.

The first part was plausible enough though, and I could tell it honestly. My appetite started to go. I would become nauseous when I ate. This didn't stop me from drinking, but it was obvious that something was wrong. I still wasn't willing to change my behavior.

I was tired all the time. Any physical activity would lead to exhaustion. I knew this wasn't normal, but if I could make it to the couch, kitchen, bathroom, and bedroom, I didn't see the need to take any action. Of course, my denial was profound. It amazes me to look back and think that I thought living like that was okay.

My belly became extended. My feet began to swell. I could not shrug the edema off as I had done with other symptoms of my illness. I gave in to my wife's urging and consulted a doctor. Unfortunately for me and my wife, he didn't diagnose the problem correctly. He became distracted by my red blood cell count. The numbers were too low for him to believe them, so he retested to rule out a lab error. The numbers came back the same, alarming the doctor. He explained my fatigue by attributing it to acute anemia. He prescribed B12 shots and diuretics for the edema.

My condition continued to worsen.

At some point he decided to refer me to Stanford Hospital and an appointment was made. One night my wife came to my bed and insisted on taking me to the emergency room. I told her I could make it to the appointment the next day. She pointed out that the appointment wasn't for another two days.

I had figured I could make it through the night, but even I wasn't certain that I could make it for two nights. I gave in. She took me to the emergency room and we were lucky that she did. I would not have otherwise made it through the night.

This is the point where my story starts to become less reliable. Less believable.

My brain was in a fog. I can now remember some things but not others. The first thing I remember? Having my belly drained of fluids. I recall the guy doing the draining being a bit amazed at how much fluid he took out.

Being in a hospital bed hooked up to IVs. Drifting in and out of consciousness. The nurses taking blood, getting it tested, putting in new IVs, taking more blood, getting it tested, putting in new IVs—a seemingly endless cycle.

I remember hating them. Why couldn't they leave me alone to get some sleep? I clearly remember thinking that. Of course, while I was resenting them, they were busy saving my life.

At some point, I lost consciousness, and this is when my story gets weird. I don't blame you if you don't believe me when I report what happened. Most people tell me that I was dreaming about what happened next, but I think it was more than a dream. I can replay it all from start to finish just by closing my eyes—something I can't do with any other dream sequence. Not even one of my old recurring nightmares.

I found myself looking down a long corridor. There was a black wall to my left and a rushing river to my right. I often wonder why I didn't turn around to see what was behind me, but it simply never entered my mind to do so. My first inclination was to move away from the river and toward the wall, but I was stunned by the freezing cold that was emanating from the wall. It was so painful that I jumped away from it and nearly tumbled into the river.

Looking into the river I knew at once that it was called The River of Forgetfulness. Other people might have called it something else, but this is what it was called in my case.

I don't know how I knew.

I simply knew.

"How bad could it be?" I wondered. "Wouldn't it be great to forget all the pain and the suffering?"

Falling into the River of Forgetfulness seemed like a good idea. I did wonder where the current would take me. I got my answer with a certainty I have no way of explaining.

The river would deposit me on an island. The island would only contain people who had been in the river. None of them could remember anything. They all wandered around with arms outstretched as if they were trying to grasp something just out of their reach. Grandparents could be next to grandchildren, and neither would recognize the other!

I wanted no part of such an island, and I recoiled from the river. The quick freeze of the wall stopped me in my tracks. It was obvious to me now that the only way out was down the corridor. I began to walk down it.

This was not a pleasant walk. Drifting too near the wall was immediately painful.

Walking too near the river was frightening. For some reason, it simply never occurred to me to stop and rest. I soldiered on with the conviction that I had to keep moving.

At some point—who knows how long I had been stumbling along—I saw a faint light ahead to the left. Redoubling my efforts, I hurried as best I could to reach the light. When I arrived at the point of origin, I was amazed to look over past the river and see my hospital room the next level up.

I saw the bed. The nurses. The IVs. What I imagined was myself in the bed.

How could I be in two places at once? There was no way to cross the river, so I eventually turned back to look at the source of the light.

The light was a gentle golden yellow and it came from a door that had a hatch you would turn to open as you would on a submarine. The light was soft and welcoming. I could hear beautiful singing coming from behind the door and was overcome with a desire to open it. Then I heard little whispers in my ear encouraging me to turn the hatch. That was my awakening.

I had heard these whispers before. I had heard them while in my bed or on my couch in the dark. They would tell me how misunderstood I was. They would console me that I was a good, kind person in a world full of insincerity and hatred.

They would tell me these sorts of things and I thought these whisperers were my friends.

Suddenly, I knew them for who they were. These were shadow whisperers. They only came out in the dark, because the daylight would expose them for the tiny, ugly things they really were. What we call shadows were just the gateways into their realm. They were not my friends. I dared not do what they urged me to do.

I then knew that the songs I was hearing were just more temptations. They too had to be resisted. As sweet as they sounded, I knew that opening the door would be a mistake. All at once, I knew what was behind the door.

There was a complete absence of warmth. A complete absence of light. The cold of the black wall was only a taste of the cold behind it. Yet creatures lived there.

Creatures that were waiting for a being of light to enter their domain. These creatures would drain you of your light and of everything else—including your rage and anger. They would leave you with nothing other than misery and despair, and then they would leave you until time itself would end.

I was not ready for that, if I ever could be. Even the River of Forgetfulness was preferable to opening that door. With all my willpower I turned to look away.

When I had managed to turn my back on the golden soft light that was a lie, I opened my eyes. I couldn't believe what I saw.

There was a bridge over the river that had not been there before. I walked back over it before it had a chance to disappear. I awoke back in my hospital bed a changed man. My spiritual awakening was complete and my journey of recovery began.

I saw the nurses for what they were. Dedicated professionals, trying to save a life that many would've thought beyond saving. I couldn't believe how ungrateful I had been. I owed my life to these people that I had earlier thought of as harpies set on torturing me while I was down. What a fool I had been.

Soon I was transferred into another room. My wife asked a nurse why, and she answered, "It's a good thing. He's off death watch." I am certain that they both had assumed that I was out cold and couldn't hear them, but I will never forget it. I didn't know there was such a thing as a "death watch." I believe it was just the nurse's way of saying that they had to be able to record my exact time of death since my death seemed entirely plausible.

I underwent further tests and procedures. The doctor came in to deliver the bad news. I would need a liver transplant, he told us. I accepted this news with equanimity. I was content with whatever my future held because I knew that it was not something I could control.

There was a visiting specialist who came in to see me, and he told me something different. He said I might or might not need a transplant and that he was referring me to another specialist he knew for whom he had high regard. He also told me that I could no longer drink. He did so by tilting his head back and pouring an imaginary bottle down into his mouth, but I got the message.

My appointment to see the specialist was shortly after my discharge. It took some time before I was ready to leave the hospital. I had lost a great deal of weight.

My strength and balance had been compromised. The highlight of my day was when my wife would come to visit, and the highlight of her day was when she got to leave!

I can still remember the time I could have chicken soup. Hospital food is rarely raved about, but this was an amazing treat for me. It tasted wonderful. It was soon topped by a serving of Jell-O. I have no words to describe how magnificent that tasted!

When I was at last walking to my appointment, I was completely calm. This is from a guy who would have panic attacks going to get his teeth cleaned. I had been changed in such a way that I no longer was worried about whether my expectations would be met, or my worst fears realized.

I no longer had expectations!

It was going to be whatever it was going to be.

The doctor was going to tell me yes or no as far as the transplant was concerned, and there was no reason to waste energy worrying about something I had no control over.

> There was no reason to waste energy worrying about something I had no control over.

After introducing himself, the doctor got straight to the point. He said, "If your numbers were any worse, I would put you on the list, but I think you can get better." I was relieved, but I was prepared to accept anything he had to tell me. I must've looked ungrateful.

He then told me that I could never drink again. I accepted this with an equanimity which he probably mistook as simply not understanding. He continued by saying, "If you drink, you will die." I still had no reaction because I had already accepted that fact.

He continued, "If you drink, you will die, and I don't mean eventually!" At that point, I must've given him the reaction he had been looking for because he moved on. In truth, I hadn't realized that it could happen so quickly, and I was mildly surprised. He felt that I finally understood.

He then told me that I needed to go to AA or see a therapist who specialized in this type of work. He was a great guy, and really helped me on my way to recovery. But he didn't know that there were other options than AA.

Obviously, a therapist would cost a significant amount of money and I wouldn't meet with them daily, so AA seemed to be the better choice between the two. I wish that I had known about other options at that time, but I did not. After some years of working with the AA program, I am fortunate to have discovered other options. These turned out to be a better fit for me. AA might very well work for you, but if it doesn't, do not give in to despair. Keep seeking the program that fits your needs. Seeking may not guarantee that you will find, but you cannot find if you do not seek.

CHAPTER FIVE

TO AA AND BEYOND

WHEN I WAS TOLD I had to go to AA, I remained unconvinced. I still had the notion that I could do it myself. My father taught me to teach myself rather than wait to be taught. I had become a chess master without ever having a coach or taking a lesson. I had accomplished many things by studying materials and becoming proficient. I assumed I could refrain from drinking by acquiring knowledge and by relying on my own willpower.

But I was in no shape to go anywhere for several weeks. I had experienced what one doctor called a rupture, and another a hernia, in the connective tissue between my liver and abdomen. Toxins the liver processes and then secretes into the abdomen for elimination were getting backed up into my liver.

This backup of toxins led to cirrhosis, liver scarring, brain fog, edema, and many other symptoms. I lost a great deal of weight and strength. My balance was severely impaired. Getting from the bed to the bathroom was my biggest daily challenge. Quality sleep was elusive even though I was virtually bedridden. I would experience waking dreams and dreamless states of unconsciousness.

When I finally began to sleep, the dreams I did have were chaotic and completely confusing. It was a long time before I was able to get a good night's sleep. The edema also took many weeks to subside. I tried to walk as much as I possibly could, but

I sometimes found my legs turning to jelly and unable to take another step.

This led to several falls and some comical faceplants. I broke my glasses more than once. I wasn't tempted to drink, so my delusion was still in place. The fact that I was still so sick that I didn't want a drink never entered my thinking. It didn't occur to me to wonder what it would be like once I began to feel better.

After I had gotten out of the hospital, many weeks went by before I decided to give AA a try. I didn't suddenly get smarter. I had an experience that made me realize that I really did need help.

I was sitting outside on a hot summer day and this thought popped into my head: One beer would taste great. I sincerely considered it. Then, I heard my doctor's voice in my ear. "You will die, and I don't mean eventually." I also realized that if I allowed myself to have one beer, it would not stop there.

I was the type of person that would naturally think that if one beer felt good, two would be better! I knew myself well enough to know that it would be off to the races the first time I had a drink. That is when I realized that I could not do it alone. To my chagrin, I would have to face the music and go to an AA meeting.

My feet were still too swollen to drive, so my wife dropped me off at my first meeting. It was one flight up and I could only manage the stairs one at a time. I even had to use the handrail to pull myself up. I collapsed into the first chair closest to the door.

There were around thirty people in the room seated around tables arranged in a horseshoe, with more seats behind them on two sides. I saw people talking and laughing together and I figured, "Great, another place I don't fit in."

Once the meeting began, I kept checking my watch. It was one of the longest hours I could ever remember. My wife wasn't going to pick me up until the end of the hour so I sat there hoping that I would survive. I am not sure whether I heard what anyone said, but people continued talking!

I wanted to escape. After the meeting was over, to my horror, people came up to me and started to introduce themselves. They were very kind and offered me things such as phone numbers and meeting schedules, but I was concentrating on not throwing up. I just wanted them to leave me alone and let me get out of there.

To say that my mindset was a healthy one would be about the biggest lie I could tell. I was so set on being miserable that I can't imagine how anyone could've made me feel welcome. They sure tried though. I decided that I would not come back.

Luckily for me, that conviction did not last. A week later I went again to the same meeting.

It was only slightly less intolerable.

It was only later that I realized that the problem wasn't the people.

I was the problem.

I found out that the people were part of the solution, and I just had to be willing to give it a try. I tried for about five years.

One reason I gave it a try was that someone said just the right thing to me at just the right time. He said, "Go to ninety meetings in ninety days, or until you start to like it."

My reaction was typical for me at the time. I thought, "I will go to ninety meetings in ninety days, and I will show you! I'll be miserable the whole time!" But he was right. Just a few weeks in, I started to like it.

I did the things they told me to do:

- I worked the steps.
- I got a sponsor.
- I went to meetings.
- I went to two book study meetings a week for three years.

I would hear people say something at every meeting that was helpful. But I would also hear something that I thought was complete malarkey. This combination of malarkey and wisdom was wearing me down. I told my sponsor that I was ready to quit. Eventually, I decided that I wasn't fit for the AA program. I was happy for the people it worked for, but I simply wasn't one of them.

My sponsor and another older fellow, whom I liked a great deal, took me aside for a pep talk. They told me that it was their experience that people who stopped going to meetings inevitably would drink again. This caused me to pause. They also told me that AA was the best program for stopping drinking, and this wasn't as easy for me to accept.

I had read *In the Realm of Hungry Ghosts* by Dr. Gabor Maté and I knew that there were other ways of dealing with addiction. One of the flaws I found in AA was the conviction that alcoholics were different from other addicts. Addicts are addicts. Sure, it can help to talk to someone who has the same addiction, but that doesn't mean you should talk to them exclusively. This only serves to hide what you have in common. I believed that speaking to only other alcoholics would be detrimental to my recovery.

Nevertheless, I allowed myself to be convinced to continue. There were some problems that I simply could not get past. Remember that *Alcoholics Anonymous* was written by a man who had served in World War I. Living through the crash of 1929 and the subsequent Depression helped him to see the world a certain way.

He had a near-death experience of the "bright light" variety that caused him to believe in a Higher Power he called God. In fact, his God was the one we associate with White Anglo-Saxon Protestants, whom we call WASPs. I was not a WASP, and I did not believe in the God that this man believed in. AA would have an out for this. They would say that it could be the God of your understanding.

Yet, in meeting after meeting, I would hear people speak about the God of this man's understanding.

He would even grant people an out by suggesting they use the group as their Higher Power if they could not accept the God of his understanding. However, it was clear to me that he believed that a "miracle" would occur, just as it did for him, and you would come to believe in the one true God.

From my perspective, this was a mid-twentieth-century program for WASPs—for male WASPs at that.

I could not understand how women and minorities could possibly buy into this program.

It turned out that a lot of them couldn't.

People in AA often would claim that AA was the most successful program for treating alcoholism. I would agree that the statement was true if you only used a certain metric. It was not true if you used others.

The total number of people that stayed sober because of the AA program was impressive. However, the retention rate was poor. According to cbtrecovery.org, the retention rate is less than 5% after one year. They had a lot of built-in reasons for why that was, but I didn't think they were taking a very honest look at themselves.

The message they were trying to advance had not kept up with the times. People in the 21st century were coming into AA with dual addictions and dual diagnoses that were far more prevalent than they were in the mid-twentieth century. The AA program was not equipped to deal with these types of individuals.

The literature was peppered with off-putting language. For a program based on attraction, they could be remarkably repulsive at times. There was even a chapter titled "To Wives" as though only husbands would be alcoholics. In that chapter, they basically said to the wife, "Honey, I'm sorry for the hell I put you through, but here is what you can do for me now."

Reading *Quit Like a Woman* by Holly Whitaker years later confirmed for me the patriarchal way of thinking of male WASPs. The AA book was indeed off-putting for many women. Whitaker offered yet another way for women to quit drinking.

Patriarchy is not the only term offensive to women. Even the use of the word "fellowship" to describe the AA community conjured images of a fraternal order. Why not use the word "kinship" instead?

Why ask a Sikh to hold hands and say the "Lord's Prayer" at the end of meetings? Why not just say the "Serenity Prayer" instead?

The change mechanism in AA is a slow and cumbersome process. Certain dogmatic and rigid belief systems are set in place that are difficult to overcome. Many of us practiced a sort of mental translation when certain things were said. We would say our own words under our breath instead of buying into the dogma. For me, this was not an honest way of participating in the meetings.

> **It was not AA that I needed. It was the sense of community that it provided.**

If I tried to express my concerns, I would meet with pushback. It took a great deal of courage to fly in the face of conventional wisdom. People would come up to me after the meeting and thank me for what I had said. They would tell me that they agreed with me but were not comfortable with confrontation.

They saw how I was treated, and wanted no part of it.

This was additional evidence, for me, that AA was not meeting the needs of many people. They simply did not know where else to turn. They were also often told that if they stopped going to meetings, they would end up drinking again.

I came to understand that it was not AA that I needed. It was the sense of community that it provided. I had learned that I could not do it alone.

Where else could I find the community except through AA?

That was the next step on my road to recovery.

I might not find it even if I sought it. I also knew that if I did not seek, I would not find.

Happily, I found what I was looking for.

CHAPTER SIX

YOGA AND THE TWELVE STEPS™

I N AA YOU ARE told that prayer and meditation are critical activities.

There is an assumption that people know how to do these things, but there is little to no training on how to acquire these skill sets.

When I tried to meditate, I found it extremely difficult. I could not seem to stop the chatter in my mind.

It turns out that this was not just a problem for me. Many people have the same difficulty. There is even a term for it, called "Monkey Mind," because it sounds like monkeys chattering when you are trying to concentrate.

I had practiced meditation when I was younger and thought it wouldn't be difficult for me to take it up again. I was wrong. I could not calm my mind. As soon as I would begin to clear my mind, a stray thought would pop into my head and distract me. This cycle of clearing and diverting was not something that I could break.

When I expressed this to a neighbor, she and my sister found someone they thought could help me. Once again, community and communication did for me what I could not do for myself. Not only did they find someone to help me, but they pestered me until I agreed to see her. That reminded me how we do not always know what is for our own good.

Further along in my recovery, I learned to take suggestions

better. What was the harm in trying? If the suggestion didn't work for me, I could always just move on to something else. I managed to overcome my initial skepticism and replace it with a sense of adventure.

The woman I was referred to went by the name of Divya, and she was part of a community called Ananda. It was a temple and teaching center in Palo Alto, California. It was also a yoga center. I agreed to go see her—albeit reluctantly. It was one of the best decisions I have ever made.

She taught me two different meditation techniques, and, with practice, I became adept at them. Meditation became a daily practice. I ended up developing my own way of meditating—without those techniques, I would never have been able to silence the Monkey Mind.

We began to discuss other topics about relaxation and calmness. I made real progress in quelling my anxiety. At her recommendation, I read *Autobiography of a Yogi* by Paramhansa Yogananda, which was an eye-opening and uplifting work for me. We continued to meet and rarely spoke about meditation. In fact, she became my Spiritual Advisor, and I still meet with her a few times a month.

> I managed to overcome my initial skepticism and replace it with a sense of adventure.

She suggested that I take a Restorative Yoga class that she had begun teaching. I, of course, met this with my usual contempt prior to investigation. I knew yoga was good for your posture and flexibility, but there were a lot of things that could be good for me—like Pilates—that I just didn't do. Although I very much wanted to say no, I had to admit that her suggestions had been good up to this point.

I said yes.

I was amazed at how much the class helped me. The injuries from my younger days of playing sports were catching up to me as I got older. These postures were gentle enough for me to do without experiencing any pain. It gave me another chance to work on my breathing and body awareness and control. The best part I learned wasn't about flexibility and improved posture at all! At least for me, it was about learning to control and move energy within my own body. The Sanskrit word for this was *prana*, but "energy" is perhaps the best word in English. This ability to control and move energy in my body was consistent with the Reiki practice that I had also been working on. Reiki is a Japanese technique of using energy to heal. I had gotten a level one certification in Reiki just about the time I tried Restorative Yoga.

It was as if an entirely new world had been opened for me. Whenever I felt anxious or agitated, I now had the tools and techniques to restore myself to a peaceful, calm place.

The key for me was to be aware that I had become anxious or agitated. Once I was aware, I knew what to do about it.

My work with Divya was really paying off when she mentioned another class that was just beginning. It was called "Yoga and the Twelve Steps™." This time, I jumped at the chance to take it. I am very grateful that I did.

The class was led by two people, Vivekadevi and Yudhisthira. Although I had been to many step study meetings in AA, what the two of them provided in this class was a much deeper dive. They helped me understand the yoga principles behind the steps, and my awareness of Vedic Indian traditions and wisdom began to stir and grow.

Not only did the course provide great insight into my own recovery, but it introduced me to the ancient wisdom and teachings of the Vedas. This is an ancient practice that was set down in Sanskrit and became the basis for Hinduism.

The most referenced scripture would probably be the *Bhagavad Gita.*

After taking this class, I read the Gita a couple of times, and listened to the audiobook. I still wasn't satisfied with my understanding of the material, so I took an online class at the Hindu

University of America. I was the only non-Indian in the class, but I got a great deal out of it. My understanding deepened.

I realized that there was nothing new in the AA literature. One of the phrases that made a deep impression on me in AA was "freedom from the bondage of self." It turned out that two thousand years earlier, Krishna had promised Arjuna "freedom from the bondage of self-will." Much wisdom had been rediscovered, but some malarkey had been added too. I was not about to become a Hindu, nor was I going to be a disciple of Yogananda, but I had been introduced to a different way of looking at what we called reality.

I was also encouraged to find my own path and walk it. I heard the words "Karma" and "Dharma" tossed around a good deal but had learned that people who used those words usually had only a superficial understanding of what they meant. I also learned that the direct translation of Sanskrit into English was often lacking. I learned from people who communicated the deeper meaning behind the words, and I was able to look at the world from a completely different perspective.

My confidence grew. I came to realize that finding my path and walking it was my duty. My path might not be another's. Even if a million people walked one path, if it was not mine to walk, I could not indulge myself in walking a path other than my own. Even if this meant that I would not fit in.

Learning to trust my own internal resonance became one of the greatest gifts I could give to myself. If the language used in a book or by another person resonated with me then it was my truth. If it did not, it was not. The answers for me were obtained by looking inward. As was often stated in AA, recovery is an inside job.

The lessons I learned from Yoga and the Twelve Steps™ resonated more deeply with me than in any of the step study meetings I had attended. The yoga principles behind the steps struck me as a deeper truth. I was rediscovering ancient truths that had been passed down for centuries by yogis and gurus far wiser than myself.

There was less dissonance than I experienced in AA. There was not the rigidity of thought and the dogma that I had been accustomed to in AA. The central idea I internalized was that I was not in the process of becoming someone new. I was in the process of recovering my sense of self. I did not have to become. I just had to be.

Being present in the moment and experiencing thoughts and emotions with detached appreciation became a daily practice. Initially, I was not good at this. Over time and with practice, I became more and more skillful. I learned to cut myself some slack when I struggled. I was only human.

The compassion and kindness that I learned to show others could also be turned inward. I did not have to hurry. I could be patient. Even though I had been impatient and hurried for decades, I could learn to change my behavior and my attitude. Any success was self-reinforcing. Any struggle was temporary.

Though I had found my path not only to recovery but also to enlightenment, I still had to manage my expectations. I was not going to become enlightened tomorrow. I could not expect myself to be. I was walking the path towards my own recovery, but I was not recovered. It would be a process.

The class itself not only presented me with new terminology and a new way of thinking about my reality, but it also provided me with a sense of community.

The teachers did an amazing job of establishing a safe environment. People felt comfortable sharing their pain and suffering in ways that society at large generally discourages.

Whether their addictions were based on food, co-dependence, or drugs (including alcohol), seemed to matter very little. We all had so much in common that it was easy to relate to one another. We inspired each other to dig deep and to keep digging to become aware of those things that were holding us back from achieving our own true selves.

In AA, I often found people confusing unity with uniformity. In this class, we were experiencing unity. We were not mirror images of one another. We often had different experiences and different types of struggles. With our teacher's help, we were able to cut through the differences and focus on the similarities in a way that I had never experienced before.

I had met individuals capable of doing this in AA, but the larger the group, the stronger the pressure was to conform. Conformity was not an issue in Yoga and the Twelve Steps™. We could celebrate our differences. Everyone was searching for their own truth. There may well be eternal truths and the class sought those. Yet the focus was on turning the gaze inward and finding the truth that resonated with our own deeper (or higher) selves. There was no judgment of others.

There was no correcting of anyone's belief system.

We are not taught how to do this in the society that I was raised in. It isn't even generally valued. However, it meant everything to me when it came to finding and walking my own path. It turned out, for me, that I did not need the approval of others.

> Relief from anxiety allowed me to make better decisions and behave in a way that was more in tune with the way I wanted to behave.

I found that I was the only one capable of knowing whether I was walking my path. I could behave in a way that was socially acceptable but was not consistent with my inner truth. This was a primary source of the anxiety that I had carried around with me all those years. Walking my own path and staying consistent even when encountering disapproval relieved me of that anxiety. I never seemed to make good decisions when I was anxious.

Relief from anxiety allowed me to make better decisions and behave in a way that was more in tune with the way I wanted to behave. This led to better outcomes.

The universe had a way of reflecting back. By way of the consequences of my actions, how much better it was to be calm before making choices. Not only my choices, but my behavior improved. My behavior had become a result of conscious decision-making rather than instinctive reactions to external events.

By regaining the power of choice and making wiser decisions, I no longer felt alienated or estranged. These feelings had been my constant companions throughout my life. Freedom from these feelings was a blessing. Even when they returned—and they did—I would see them for what they were: impermanent. Whenever I became agitated or anxious—and I did—I could become aware of this state, in the moment, and employ the tools and techniques I had learned to recover my sense of well-being and ease.

This may not work for everyone, but it worked for me.

The goal is to find what works for you.

The measure of what works for you is your own sense of well-being and ease. If you try a program that leaves you anxious and agitated, it might not help you find your own path. Keep seeking one that will. It is unlikely that you will be able to find it on your own. I certainly was not able to do it, and I tried.

The sense of community, when you find it, will help you during the struggles that inevitably will come. Even when you find your path and begin to walk it, it will not be easy.

No one told me that this was going to be easy. I established a daily ritual for myself that got me grounded, calm, and connected first thing in the morning. I learned that I had to do this every morning. If I took a day off, I might take two. Soon I would not be doing the work at all. It was critical that I did it every day so that my habit of finding excuses not to do it would be overridden by the force of habit. I learned not to tell myself I had to do it forever. That sounded too heavy. I just had to do it every day.

The spiritual rituals that I performed worked for me. I had not been taught them by anyone else, and I did not find them in a book or online. I developed them through a process of trial and error. If it felt right, I kept it. If it did not serve, I discarded it. I discovered what worked for me.

The process rather than the specific practice is what is important. What works for me may not work for anyone else. I had to be connected to the inner resonance to feel my way towards what did and did not work. It was a process that emerged over time. Not only did I continue to add and subtract rituals, but I modified them as time went on. My inner resonance was always my guide.

This was a process of discovery—and that discovery felt wonderful. Every morning I would wake up one way and by practicing my spiritual rituals I would transform myself into a different state of being. It was a state of being that was happy and content. I would start the series of rituals by saying, "I have work to do."

It always felt like work. But the hard part was just getting started. I had to overcome what I called Dark Inertia. Once I got going it would just flow from one ritual to the next. When I was done, I would wonder why I thought of it as work at all! Yet, the next morning it would feel like work again. The Dark Inertia had to be overcome again and again.

With time, my confidence in my ability to overcome the Dark Inertia grew.

I did not let it discourage me.

I simply needed to get into action.

CHAPTER SEVEN

BUDDHIST-BASED RECOVERY

I regularly attended two Buddhist-based recovery programs: "Refuge Recovery" and "Recovery Dharma." I can only speak to those programs I was directly involved in, but there may indeed be others.

Buddhism provides a non-theist approach to recovery. It accepts, as fact, that pain and suffering are part of the human condition. It provides a path to freedom from suffering. This was a path set out by Siddhartha Gautama, who lived during the 5th or 6th century BCE and came to be known as the Buddha.

I was first introduced to this wisdom when as a young man, I read the novel *Siddhartha* by Herman Hesse. It tells of a spiritual journey towards self-discovery, and I loved it. Even if this is not your path, there is great wisdom to be found in these teachings.

Reading a variety of books by the Dali Lama over the years kept me in touch with Buddhism, which always had an appeal to me. More recently, the book *Why Buddhism Is True* by Robert Wright reinforced my previous attraction to this spiritual practice.

Of course, I had not heard about any Buddhist-based recovery programs. It was only by chance that I heard about "Refuge Recovery" from a friend in AA.

She had gone to some meetings and was very enthusiastic. I checked online and found that a meeting was held every week near where I lived.

I started attending regularly and enjoyed it. The man who led the meeting began by stating that he was not a Buddhist teacher. This helped set the tone for a peer-to-peer discussion session where everyone was a part-time teacher and part-time student.

I really enjoyed these meetings.

Then the pandemic hit.

Meetings went online. I helped provide service by managing some Zoom meetings in AA until things were pretty much under control. I then looked for Refuge Recovery meetings online. I found quite a few.

It was only after attending a series of online meetings that I learned about Recovery Dharma. Apparently, there had been a split between the two organizations prior to my getting involved. Refuge Recovery followed the teaching of Noah Levine and used his book *Refuge Recovery* as the primary means of teaching a Buddhist approach to recovery. I found a wonderful community there. They used the word *Sangha* to describe this community, and people talked openly about their struggles and their progress.

Although the endgame was enlightenment, there was no real expectation that anyone would become enlightened in the same manner as Siddhartha. It was all about progress along the path to enlightenment. This was entirely consistent with my own approach and with the Vedic teachings that I had immersed myself in previously.

The presence of many people who had a twelve-step background was clear. Over and over again, I would hear someone say that they had tried AA, but that it hadn't worked for them. Since that had been my own experience, I felt like I fit.

After a few months, I noticed some difficulties. There seemed to be an overreliance on one person, Noah Levine. I found Noah to be an open and willing listener, not overly interested in establishing any kind of group-think. Unfortunately, some groups practiced that despite his best intentions.

I found people saying, "Noah said," as if this would end any discussion. Rather than struggling to find how the practice of Buddhist principles applied in their lives, they seemed to be looking for a preordained solution that they could follow, and they were looking to Noah for the answers. I was not comfortable with that.

Noah didn't encourage this type of thinking. In fact, he discouraged it. It just seemed to be a natural tendency for some people to behave in this manner.

That reminded me of the rigidity of thought I had experienced in AA. In that program, people often cited Bill Wilson (Bill W.) as the ultimate authority. I never understood that. Bill Wilson was a good salesman, but not exactly a model character. His philandering ways were common knowledge. The main takeaway for me was not to engage in any kind of hero worship nor to entrust your thinking to another.

There seemed to be, through no apparent fault of Noah's, too much of that going on in Refuge Recovery. So, I started attending Recovery Dharma meetings. Right away I heard things that made me more comfortable.

The meetings were peer-led and they followed no one individual's teachings. They were there to understand the "Four Noble Truths" and the "Eightfold Path" of Buddhism. I loved the emphasis on peer-to-peer teaching and learning. We can all learn from one another, and we all have something to offer.

Another point of emphasis was on empowerment. I had found the emphasis on powerlessness in AA to be doing much more harm than good. I was fully on board with the idea of empowering each other to be the best we could be.

All beings have the power and potential to free themselves from suffering.

We just can rarely, if ever, do it by ourselves.

We need a community.

Another concept that both AA and Refuge Recovery shared was the idea of sponsorship (AA) or mentoring (Refuge). That can be good but might lead to a hierarchical relationship that I considered unhealthy. When done correctly, it is a wonderful thing. When done incorrectly, it can be quite damaging. I never wanted to put myself in the situation of knowing more than someone else did. It could be a trap for someone such as myself.

Showing someone the ropes was another thing entirely. Helping someone find the resources that they didn't know existed was a helpful service to provide. Lending an ear could also be a wonderful service. Making someone feel that they are not alone was a gift. When I gave this gift, I would get back more in return. The mutual sense of belonging and being connected was always uplifting and beneficial.

Another thing that AA and Refuge Recovery had in common was the self-description of their programs as abstinence-based. That can lead to superficial thinking. Abstinence may be a result of your spiritual practice, but it can never be the basis for it. "Renunciation" is a far better word to use, in my opinion. It is the giving up on worldly attachments in order to achieve spiritual liberation. If you practice renunciation, abstinence follows.

Abstinence is passive. You do not do something.

Renunciation is active. You choose to renounce a behavior and all that it implies.

I found abstinence to be fragile. Renunciation was more lasting.

I had a discussion with Noah about this topic, and I found him open to further examination of the concept. He seemed to genuinely consider my input but was not quite convinced. Of course, that was fine.

Recovery Dharma placed what I thought was the proper emphasis on renunciation, which included the intention to practice abstinence when possible. Obviously, you cannot abstain from food if that is the source of your addiction, but it is entirely possible to establish boundaries regarding what you choose to consume.

The peer-to-peer learning in Recovery Dharma was much more along the lines of how I wanted to continue to practice my recovery. Recovery Dharma was far less structured than Refuge Recovery and some people need structure. So do not be overly influenced by my preferences.

Both programs emphasize Buddhist practices. There is a fountain of wisdom to be found in either program. What works for me may not work for you, and vice-versa. The important thing is to keep seeking until you find what works for you.

It is important to also give any program a fair shot. If I quit any program at the first sign of cognitive dissonance, I would never have made the progress that I have made. Yes, I felt like quitting AA many times, but the people are what mattered to me. On any given week I might go to meetings in all three programs.

All the programs I have been involved in have something to offer. My personal favorite remains the classes I have been taking in Yoga and the Twelve Steps™, but, currently, that is not always available. Hopefully, that will change at some point in the future and these sessions may be more widely available.

> The important thing is to keep seeking until you find what works for you.

Both Refuge Recovery and Recovery Dharma state that other programs are available. This is a far more encouraging and enlightened point of view. Only AA seems married to the idea that its program is the best. I had to overcome my distaste for this lack of humility so I could profit from the benefits it offers.

I often encounter people who give up too quickly. At the first sign of relapse, they become discouraged. The tendency to give in to despair seems to be ingrained in the addict's mind. This is when they need to be empowered most. People need to feel worthy, or they begin again the spiral downward into incomprehensible demoralization.

Perseverance is required. Many people do not believe they have what it takes. It is challenging. It can be exhausting. That's why a community is vital. Whether it is in AA, Refuge Recovery, or Recovery Dharma, the community can lift you up when you are at your lowest.

It has been my experience that ancient wisdom is what best fits me. The trick is to adapt it to our times. People must learn how to apply this wisdom to their lives as they live it today. It is important to be part of a community and to learn from each other how modern stresses lead us away from our chosen path.

In the past, a grandparent's experience was often like the grandchildren's experience. The rate of change in society today has accelerated. The experience of the young person today may contain stresses that the grandparent never had to face. Bullying on social media is just one example.

Ancient wisdom is still applicable, but the adaptation to the present reality needs to be learned. Younger people coming into the meetings today often find their reality is not valued by older generations. It is often dismissed. They leave feeling alienated and misunderstood.

However, there are always some people in any program I have been a part of that can translate their experience into today's reality. These are the true elder statesmen. They don't try to fit square pegs into round holes. They find a common ground and convey their knowledge and experience to the newcomer.

This is an invaluable skill set, and not everyone has it.

Even if you are put off at first, as I was, consider continuing to go back. You may eventually find someone who says something that relates directly to your experience. It doesn't have to be the same experience. I tried to focus on the similarities rather than the differences—I could usually find them.

Buddhism has a wide range of leniency for the precise way to practice its teachings. Just as with meditation itself, there are more ways to do it right than some people will lead you to believe. I had to hang in there until I was able to discover or invent what worked for me.

I will close this chapter by sharing the "Four Noble Truths" as I have learned them.

If you are interested in learning more about them or "The Eightfold Path," just find a Buddhist-based meeting online or near you.

The Four Noble Truths and the corresponding commitments:

1. There is suffering. We commit to understanding the truth of suffering.
2. There is a cause of suffering. We commit to understanding that craving leads to suffering.
3. There is an end to suffering. We commit to understanding and experiencing that less craving leads to less suffering.
4. There is a path that leads to the end of suffering. We commit to cultivating the path.

CHAPTER EIGHT

POWER

P OWER.
Some seek it. Some recoil from it.
Few really understand it.

As always, it depends on how you define your terms, but most people have some sort of concept about an ultimate source of power.

The question of power is always an interesting one. In AA this power is called God. The idea expressed often is to "let go and let God." This idea never sat well with me. I never had a problem with a power greater than myself. Doing a tackling drill in high school with our Allstate fullback had cured me of any delusions about that!

Just because I was not the most powerful being in the world did not mean that I was powerless. I did not expect anyone to do anything for me, including a Supreme Being. This was both a credit and a debit in my accounting system. It was good that I took personal responsibility for my own behavior, but it was not so good that I thought I could do everything myself. Everybody needs help sometimes and I was lying to myself to think that I never did.

But what would an objective view of power look like? Many people in AA took their understanding of their power from the first step:

1. We admitted we were powerless over alcohol, and that our lives had become unmanageable.

Notice that it says we were. It does not say we are. Yet people in AA continue to express their powerlessness over alcohol in the present as well as in the past tense. I did not understand this. I had regained the power of choice, and I chose to renounce alcohol.

Alcohol had no power over me. It did when I was in the throes of my addiction, but that was no longer the case. Alcohol, to me, was a powerless inert liquid and nothing more. It had no kinetic energy; it only had potential energy if I chose to imbibe it.

This did not give me a false sense of security. I knew very well that if I chose to drink again, I would end up surrendering my power of choice. I would be at the mercy of cravings that I would be powerless to resist.

However, I had no intention of surrendering my power of choice. This power was freely given to me. Yes, I had squandered it in the past. But that was my past. It was not my present.

I had confidence in myself.

Confidence is not arrogance. If you express confidence in AA you can expect to be chided for being arrogant. This type of chiding is not empowerment. I encourage people to be self-confident. I found many who have had their confidence shaken. It serves no purpose to tell them that they are powerless too! What they really need is to have their confidence restored.

I also found many people in AA suffering from the conviction that they were victims. Telling them that they were powerless played right into their delusion. This gave them the feeling that they were not responsible for what had happened to them, and that could give them some sense of relief. But it did not give them confidence.

Many were still tormented by the feeling that they were never safe. They were not taught to take responsibility for their own actions but to buy into the sense that they had no control over their own lives. Things they had no control over happened to them. This was sometimes true, but it often wasn't. Taking responsibility for your own actions, including the need to set healthy boundaries, took a back seat to this sense of powerlessness.

This type of recovery was fragile. It was only by developing a sense of confidence, and a wise differentiation between those things you could control versus those things that you could not, that their sobriety could be on more solid ground.

Human beings are not powerless over people, places, and things. They often cannot control them. That realization made a world of difference to me. How could anyone change the things they can if they were powerless? It made no sense to me.

Understanding that I could not control things and that I could not force the outcomes that I wanted were major realizations for me. Accepting those facts provided peace and serenity. Others in the AA

> **Learning to accept feelings is a time-honored way to get out of the vicious cycle of repeated relapses.**

community suffered from the need to control things. I did not, at first, realize that I was one of them. It makes no sense to tell people who have been controlling for most of their lives that they are powerless.

They know that it is simply not true.

When you try to control people, places, and things, you are often successful.

When you are unsuccessful, however, you may experience pain and suffering.

Many alcoholics who are unable to control things they expect to control experience difficulties remaining sober. The key is to help them realize that they have no right to control others. Even if they assume the right to do so, they will, almost always, eventually experience failure.

The inability to accept failure is often what drives addicts into relapse. They wish to escape the feelings associated with failure and they try to change the way they feel. Learning to accept feelings—whether good, bad, or otherwise—is a time-honored way to get out of the vicious cycle of repeated relapses.

This is not a question of powerlessness.

FREEDOM

It is a question of determining what you can or cannot change. This does not come overnight for the addict. Some of us think we cannot change anything, and others of us believe we can change everything! What is needed is a sense of balance. Achieving this balance rarely comes easily.

The other realization that was essential for me on my path to recovery was the idea of detachment. When I was attached to expectations or desires, I would frequently encounter difficulties. I was not very skillful at meeting these difficulties in a healthy way.

When my ego was running the show, I always seemed to end up in the same place. I would spiral down into a sense of worthlessness when I failed. I would get wrapped up in an exaggerated sense of my own capabilities when I succeeded. It is often said that addicts are egomaniacs with inferiority complexes. I could relate to that!

Once you experience this sense of freedom you never want to surrender it again.

The way I learned to take the wheel back from my ego was to detach from it. In yoga, this was called being in "Witness Mode." You could step back and observe your own behavior as if you were an objective third party. This was a way of freeing yourself from the ego's expectations and desires. Once you experience this sense of freedom you never want to surrender it again.

This freedom is empowering. If you are both empowered and detached, you can choose how you want to behave. You are no longer at the mercy of what your ego wants. You can see your instinctual response before you indulge it, and you can choose to behave in a different way.

This sense of freedom is self-reinforcing. The more you do it, the more you want to do it. Instead of escalating tensions, you can ease them. Your new actions produce more positive results than your old ones did.

You experience the power of choice. All beings have the

58

power and potential to free themselves from the pain and suffering caused by addiction. Where does this power come from? It comes from within.

All beings are born with an innate sense of wisdom, along with our instinctual desires. Society has a mechanism for curbing our striving to meet some of these instinctual desires and reinforcing others. What society wants is not always the best.

Rather than try to meet society's expectations, I had to learn what worked for me.

Did my behavior make me feel anxious or agitated? That was a red flag and needed further scrutiny.

Did it make me feel calm and serene? That was something worth paying attention to.

The only valid judge of how I felt was myself. Not my ego. My inner self. This inner resonance was my only true guide. I had to learn to get in touch with it and not allow my ego to interfere and alter my perceptions. My ego would—if given the slightest opportunity to do so.

Meditation and spiritual rituals were my tools for getting in touch with my inner self. The more I did them the easier it got. Certainly, some days I did better than others. But if I persevered, I could manage to get there.

What is this inner self?

Different people will use different words to describe it. I knew it when I got connected to it. It was an entirely different experience than being ego-centered. I felt a connection to something else. After long periods of meditation, I was able to put into words what the experience was like for me.

It became clear to me that I was a physical manifestation of something greater.

My identification was no longer with my body or my mind, but with something that my body and mind were a part of. I did not know this, so much as feel it.

I felt centered. I felt connected. Connected to what? Connected to all beings everywhere. This was the true source of my power, though it was not my power at all. I was merely a channel for it.

When I got connected to my inner self, I was able to channel wisdom that my own brain did not possess. Many belief systems explain how this works. Consider yourself blessed if you find one that works for you.

It was not necessary to explain how it worked. I just needed to recognize that it did work for me.

When I could quiet my mind, and make a conscious connection to this inner self, which was connected to things beyond my own being, I found answers that would otherwise have escaped me. This was a source of innate wisdom that I believe we are all born with, a gift freely given to us.

In our society, we are not trained on how to access this innate wisdom. Prayer and meditation are two practices that can help. Consider yourself fortunate if you have been trained in those areas. But your work is not yet complete. You must also recognize when that connection has been made.

You're the only one who can make that determination. Others can give external approval of your behavior and believe you have changed, but that is not necessarily confirmation. Addicts learn to mimic the behavior that society expects from them and can do a wonderful job of seeming as though they have truly changed. They can do this again and again and again.

They can lose the trust of their loved ones through these repeated betrayals.

They can lose all semblance of their self-esteem because they really thought they had changed. Some are more cynical than others, but many really believe they have made an honest attempt to change. They can be crushed to discover that they are right back where they were, behaving exactly as they did before.

This is because we may have spent our entire lives disconnected from our core being. We may have become trapped in the wants and desires of our egos. Our instinctual needs are combined with the demands that are ego-based and we find ourselves lost, unable to control our own behavior.

Even when we practice prayer and meditation, we may not make the connection to our core being.

It is important not to give into despair. Sustained effort is the answer.

Keep trying.

Pay attention.

Concentrate.

Silence the Monkey Mind.

Learn the tools that help you along the way.

I had to be honest with myself. Was I truly calmer afterward? Was I more serene? I could not lie to myself if I truly wanted to make progress. This is easier said than done, but the rewards are greater than I could have possibly imagined.

If you have spent your life in a constant state of anxiety or in a comfortable numbness through self-medication, the feelings of peace and serenity may feel foreign at first. I can remember trying for several minutes to put a name to the feeling I was experiencing. Finally, I realized that I was happy.

Do not despair. Even if it has been a long time since you have experienced happiness, calmness, and contentment, these feelings can be yours again. They have returned to me.

The more I explored this connection to what I called my core being, the more discoveries I made. This was the true source of my power—the ability to channel the collective wisdom and force for good. That power was present all around me and had been throughout the ages.

This was not my power to obtain my own wants and desires. This was a power that flowed through me and produced better behavior and results than my mind could devise on its own. I believe this is the kind of power people call divine.

Connecting to this inner power takes work. We may have to discard a lot of habitually ingrained attitudes and assumptions. We must be open to the process of discovery. There is no short-cut or way around doing the work this entails.

It may involve trial and error.

We must keep trying even when our results are not immediate or sufficiently gratifying. We must trust that the payoff will be down the road if we keep pursuing it. I call this walking my path.

Things got easier for me, but not overnight. Progress would seem slow or even nonexistent at times. But my progress was undeniable. I would feel myself calming down. I sensed when the connection was just around the corner.

When you do connect to your core being the feeling cannot be dismissed. It will be unmistakable. You may just get near it, or feel that you are close, but not quite yet connected. With perseverance you will have this experience. Once you get it, you will know it. No one will be able to deny it or take it away from you. This is what it feels like to be empowered. This is what power means to me.

You will never feel powerless again. You will know that whatever happens, you have the awareness and the tools to deal with it. These are not the unskillful defensive mechanisms of the past. Once connected, you will never feel alone again. Even if you are by yourself, you will know—down to your core being—you are never truly alone.

CHAPTER NINE

THE GOD QUESTION

O NE OF THE BIGGEST issues AA faces is their emphasis on God. Many people drop out because of it. Some don't even give it a chance because they assume it is a cult.

In my experience, AA is not a cult at all. There are, however, cultists in AA.

The word "God" means many things to many people. Reading the AA literature, I got the distinct impression that the God mentioned there was the God of White Anglo-Saxon Protestants (WASPs).

Bill Wilson, the author of *Alcoholics Anonymous*, was a believer in that God. He suffered a near-death experience and saw a blinding white light. He interpreted that as a God moment and credited it for his spiritual awakening.

Modern science now believes that this experience can be explained by a REM intrusion, according to a study by Professor Kevin Nelson of the University of Kentucky, Lexington.[1] This doesn't happen every time someone has a near-death experience. But this reported "white light" phenomenon has happened enough to pass into folklore.

If you want to believe, as Bill Wilson did, that this is a sign from God, that is your right. It is my view that this can be

---

1   Nelson KR. From the stillness of feigning death to near-death experience? *Brain Commun.* 2021 Jun 22;3(3):fcab138. doi: 10.1093/braincomms/fcab138. PMID: 34240054; PMCID: PMC8260962.

explained by earthly means. The point worth paying attention to is the spiritual awakening Bill attributed to it.

This does not mean you have to believe in God the same way Bill Wilson did. To have a spiritual awakening does not mean you have to believe in any kind of god at all. People might be confused by that, but it seems straightforward to me.

The Buddhist approach to recovery is non-theistic, but is deeply spiritual in nature. The AA approach did not work for me at all, so my own approach to the God question is quite different.

When AA was being formed, there was reportedly some discussion about this. They chose to modify the word "God" to say, "the god of your understanding." This didn't make much sense to me. Who understands God? But I was willing to give them a pass on that, as it just seemed like a bit of unskillful writing.

Bill Wilson even gives people a way to deal with the God question without accepting his own belief. He states that the newcomer to recovery could always accept the group's conscience as their higher power. The caveat is that he was expecting them to wait until a miracle occurred, as it did for him, and they would then accept the God of his understanding.

Of course, this is my interpretation of what I read and heard. But it is an interpretation shared by many others. That is why I stress finding what works for you. Pay attention to whether what people say resonates within you. If it does, I would encourage you to investigate it further. If it does not, I would suggest continuing your own personal search for what resonates as the truth for you.

You may not be able to trust this inner resonance at first. You may not even be able to identify it. This is something that might develop over time. The first order of business is to allow any toxins to exit your system. Even then, it is wise to avoid jumping to conclusions or rushing to any judgments.

Give yourself time to sort things out. There are no bonus points for getting there more quickly than anyone else. Those who arrive will get there at their own pace and time. This is when patience is a virtue.

I will share my perspective now, but it is only my own. It is no more or less valid than anyone else's. I am not trying to convince anyone to believe as I do.

The important thing is to find something that works for you. I have no way of knowing what that might be for you, but I can tell you what works for me.

The word "eternity" has often been on my mind. Ever since I was a child, I have toyed around with the meaning of the word. I can recall a conversation with my father when the subject came up. I had asked him to explain to me how God could be eternal if time itself had a beginning and an end. I have no idea how I had come to that conclusion, but I had.

I still recall his reply, "God exists outside of time." These words seemed very wise to me, but I had to think about them long and hard before I caught a glimmer of understanding. "What is outside of time?" I asked myself.

I then got a very clear image of God (an old white man with a long white beard) holding his finger out and time flowing out from his finger. This may have been a very childlike perspective, but it was deeply satisfying.

It wasn't too long afterward that I gave up on this image. I found the idea that God looked like a human being to be preposterous. I began to wonder what it meant to be made in his image. I realized that it didn't have to be taken literally.

For many years, I was comfortable with just not knowing. I didn't have to have a replacement theory in place to disagree with what others told me was their understanding. Over time, I learned that I didn't have to even argue the point.

Whatever anyone else believed was fine with me. It didn't mean I had to buy into it. Later, when I was in recovery, I learned to be happy for them. I could be happy they found something that worked for them.

It was my job to figure out what worked for me. The Sanskrit saying that I adopted was "Neti, Neti." Not this, not that. While I was searching, I did not have to accept anything that I did not feel an internal resonance with. I was also willing to be patient. My answers would come when they came, and not before.

My answers began to emerge after I took a course in quantum mechanics in the Continuing Education program at Stanford University. My first struggle was with what was referred to as synchronicity at a distance. Two quantum particles might be entangled by, for example, having their spin in synch. This seemed perfectly normal when the particles were in close contact.

Yet, it was demonstrated that when the particles were separated, and one of their spins changed, the other's spin would also change so that they stayed in synch. How could this possibly be true?

It occurred to me that they were being separated in only one way. Distance.

What if they were connected in a different way? What if we just didn't understand how they were connected?

This helped me understand that being created in God's image did not mean the image we understood. What if we were created in a way that was in an image we just didn't understand? What if that image was pure energy?

This led me back to thinking of eternity in a new way. What if it wasn't an image of a God that was eternal? What if it was simply energy that I didn't fully understand? This resonated inwardly and was deeply satisfying to me.

I started to think in terms of the Field of Eternal Energy (FEE) and thought more about what that implied. As quantum mechanics teaches, energy and matter are the same. They are simply different manifestations of the same thing. If you had energy, you had matter, even if it was only at the quantum level.

So, if energy was eternal, then matter was eternal. Matter appears all the time at the quantum level. Not out of nothing, but out of energy. If energy and matter are eternal, there is no limit to how much there is of either one. There is no constraint because there is no space or time that would constrain them. Space and time had yet to have been created.

So, when matter appears out of energy in the FEE, what form does it take?

Obviously, an entire atom does not appear all at once. Nor do the sub-nuclear particles, like protons, neutrons, and electrons. These sub-nuclear particles seem to be made from what scientists call quarks. But there are a variety of quarks. There are up, down, strange, and charmed quarks, as well as others. What are quarks made from?

The best current theory is that they are made from what scientists call strings.

These are not necessarily strings that start at point A and end at point B. They may be a circle. One thing seems certain: they vibrate.

The way I imagined it happening in my own thought experiments is that energy would convert into strings of various lengths, vibrating at various frequencies and intensities. In the FEE, these strings would appear so often and in so many varieties that they would inevitably include one vibrating at an intensity and frequency at nearly unimaginable levels.

Such a string might explode. Such an explosion might cause an unimaginable amount of energy to be produced. Of course, this would not tip the scales or make any difference in the FEE itself. If you already have an infinite amount, you cannot add to it.

But, within the FEE, this explosion might create what could be described as a Big Bang. At this time both space and time would come into existence. They would still be embedded in the FEE, but they could potentially cause a sort of bubble in the FEE that might be called a universe.

The creation of this universe did not require any intelligence or consciousness to make it happen. It just needed energy and matter to exist for eternity. If it could happen once, it would happen more than once. It could happen an infinite number of times. That's what it takes to wrap your mind around words such as "eternity."

These universes, or bubbles, would never encounter one

another. There is no space in the FEE. They would exist entirely independently. Each one could be very, very different.

Some of these explosions might be too small to lead to universes that continue to exist. They may collapse back into the FEE itself sooner rather than later. Some may reach a stasis, and others might continue to expand. There is no telling which kind of universe the one we live in is. At least, not yet.

Our universe was created by an immense, but not an infinite, amount of energy.

This energy caused matter to come into being right from the beginning of the universe's time. Time, space, and matter all began to exist in this universe, along with this immense amount of energy, because of this explosion in the FEE. The rest of the universe's history can be explained by physics, except for one thing.

Physics does not consider that the universe is embedded in the FEE. Until it does, there will always be questions that befuddle scientists. There will seem to be too much energy—or energy that can be detected but not explained.

Physics has a hard time accepting that the bubble (that we call the universe) is not all there is.

If this is the way the universe was created, there is no need for a god or supernatural being to explain the way things are.

There is no reason to ask ourselves, "Why?"

It just is.

This is a source of comfort for me, but I understand that it can be disquieting for others. If there is no God, how do we justify any sense of morality? Well, it seems to me that what is life-affirming is good. But more to the point, what is consistent with the flow of the universe is good.

To understand what that flow is and what is consistent with it, we need to go back to where it all began. Vibrations. It turns out that everything vibrates.

These vibrations may be felt, heard, or otherwise sensed. Sometimes they can be sensed in ways that conventional wisdom does not allow for.

I think this is what the yogis and mystics have been trying to teach us. Just as particles can communicate with one another at a distance, we can communicate with one another in unconventional ways. Even if we do not fully understand these ways, they are still real. It is a nature of that reality that is easy for us to ignore.

We don't live in a society of yogis and mystics. We live in a society that does not train people in their teachings. We live in a society that agrees upon what our senses tell us is real and dismisses anything else as irrelevant.

It is difficult to live in a society that routinely contradicts the very essence of what helped me to recover. I had to learn to not only accept the society I lived in but to be grateful for it. Everyone was doing the best that they could.

Yes, most people live lives of quiet desperation, but my preaching to them would not be of any service. I just had to continue to walk my path and help those that came into my sphere of influence if they desired it.

My job, as I understood it, was to flow along with the rhythm of the universe. When I could vibrate at the intensity and frequency that the cosmos vibrated at, I experienced peace and serenity. If I was too high, or too low, pain and suffering would follow. This was easier to understand intellectually than it was to live out!

It was important for me to abandon the Mr. Fix-it attitude that I had subconsciously developed. It would be the height of arrogance for me to assume that I could fix anyone else, or that they needed fixing at all.

When I stayed on my path and was in touch with the inner resonance that guided my behavior, I often found myself easing the pain and suffering of others. This felt so natural, so in tune with my purpose in life, that it was a source of encouragement even in my lowest hours.

I could not always be walking my path and in tune with the inner resonance that connected me to forces beyond myself. I don't think I have ever been able to string together twenty-four hours in a row in that state. This is when I must show the compassion to myself that I freely show to others. I am only human.

Managing my expectations and forgiving myself when I am not perfectly spiritual twenty-four-seven has been a key to my recovery. I was not yet an enlightened soul. Yet the moments of joy that I experienced when helping ease the pain and suffering of others were nothing short of divine.

It was clear to me that if I could experience these divine states, even if they were impermanent, others could as well. If I could help them experience what I had experienced, why wouldn't I?

CHAPTER TEN

WHAT IT'S LIKE NOW

Today, my life is one of always ascending plateaus of greater happiness.

Do you believe me?

No?

Good, you shouldn't.

Of course, my life today is filled with ups and downs, but my equanimity is nothing like it was. I can remain calm even in difficult situations.

I still can get anxious, agitated, or lose my temper. I am no saint. Yet, I can recover my equanimity more often and more quickly than I ever could in the past.

This has been a blessing.

Incorporating meditations and spiritual practices in my daily life reminds me of who I am, and who I want to be. I developed my own spiritual practices but you can use any meditation technique—or none. But, as always, find what works for you.

It has been my practice to begin my rituals while going for a morning walk. Again, you can do that in a sacred place you have at home, or anywhere you find that gets you in the proper frame of mind. I always begin by saying, "Dear SAME, thank you for reminding me that I have work to do."

The acronym SAME stands for Source and Mother Earth. The Source refers to the source of the cosmic vibration I wish to attune to. Mother Earth is the local source of the life-affirming energy that I also want to tap into.

After being reminded that I have work to do, I can begin my walk and my first set of spiritual rituals. This set includes the following:

1. I admit to myself that I have experienced and caused needless pain and suffering by squandering the power freely given to me.
2. I have come to believe in forces beyond my control that could ease pain and suffering.
3. I make a conscious decision to attune the power freely given to me with those forces beyond my control, to ease pain and suffering.

The steps in this set require my undivided attention. If my mind wanders, I start over. I rarely have had to start over more than one time. This requires discipline. Discipline can be developed. Do not tell yourself that you don't have it. Make up your mind to acquire it. It is a skill like any other.

> **It is important not to compare your progress with anyone else's.**

This is not a competition. Some people require more work to acquire a skillset than others. Just keep making progress. If you can look back after a couple of weeks of trying and see that you have made progress, then you are on the right track. As addicts, we tend to give up too soon. Perseverance and discipline can be developed over time.

It is important not to compare your progress with anyone else's. This is not a race. We also must show mercy to ourselves because we almost never make as much progress as we expect ourselves to. If we lower our expectations and become satisfied with merely observing our progress, without judging it, we will make our paths easier to walk.

Before I begin the next set of spiritual rituals, I say, "Dear SAME, thank you for reminding me to surrender to the moment, and to be fully present." Just as reminding myself that I have work to do helps me achieve the mindset I need to do the first set of rituals, this reminds me to do a reset before I begin the next.

I can tell whether I have surrendered to the moment. I can tell when I am fully present. I can also tell when I lie to myself and pretend that I have when I haven't. I call this "mailing it in." Yes, I have mailed it in on occasion. Try to recognize that as soon as possible, but be forgiving towards yourself when you do.

When I am certain that I have established the right frame of mind, I begin the second set.

1. Dear SAME, thank you for reminding me to forgive Trump today.
2. Dear SAME, thank you for reminding me to be loving and kind. (I repeat this until I feel it.)
3. Dear SAME, thank you for reminding me to feel fortunate for my marriage to Sheri.
4. Dear SAME, thank you for reminding me to be open to revelations.
5. Dear SAME, thank you for reminding me to Renounce and Rejoice. (I repeat this three times.)
6. Dear SAME, thank you for reminding me to understand, rather than to be understood, to understand.
7. Dear SAME, thank you for reminding me to ease pain and suffering, ease pain and suffering, ease pain and suffering.
8. Dear SAME, thank you for reminding me to have gratitude, to feel fortunate, and to be grateful.

Each of these rituals was a product of trial and error. I added some and discarded others when they no longer served. I modified them over time. For example, I began by saying, "Dear SAME, thank you for reminding me not to hate Trump today." This was a response to my feelings when listening to him pit people against other people. I found myself hating him for doing this, but I knew that hatred was only harming me. I needed to find a way to stop.

Though this worked for a while, it wasn't very satisfying. Not hating wasn't the answer. I had to find it within myself to forgive him. I was able to find the compassion I needed by concentrating on his own pain and suffering. He was clearly a man in pain.

It took a week or two, but I experienced an enormous sense of relief when I was able to forgive him. There was no longer the sense that something was pressing down on my chest and hindering my ability to breathe normally.

It was my first genuine experience of the power of forgiveness. The forgiveness I had done in the past was like brushing away a mosquito. I usually minimized how much it was bothering me, and I did nothing to prevent it from returning.

Not only did my forgiving the man ease my personal distress, but it also prevented it from coming back when I saw him on the news. I would see his pain and suffering. I could feel compassion for him. It was much easier going through life not being triggered by an image on a television screen!

This was perhaps the most dramatic of the modifications I made, but it was not the only one. I will continue to add and discard rituals. I only need to practice that which serves a need. I also will always need to be reminded of certain things. Every day is different. These rituals help me start each new day the same way.

The last spiritual ritual I apply every morning is a meditation practice.

It is connecting to each of my chakras and awakening them.

After I have returned home from the walk, I face the East. I begin by saying, "Dear Source." But this time I stop and picture the Source. My breath is slow and rhythmic. I have my eyes closed and lift my gaze off into the distance. When I can picture the energy flowing from the Source and connecting to what yogis call the "third eye," I guide it down my spine and connect it to Mother Earth. Then, I say, "And Mother Earth."

I don't say the words audibly; they sound quite distinct in my head. I then continue, picturing the energy flowing through me down to Mother Earth's core.

I say, "Mother Earth, your core is molten iron, and the color I connect to you with is red." These visualizations are an important part of my meditative practice, but they do not have to be part of yours.

"Red is the color that grounds me to you," I say, and I picture the color of red flowing up and through the sole of my left foot. I picture it rising to meet my tailbone. I repeat, "Red is the color that grounds me to you," as I see it swirling around my tailbone, down my right leg, and through the sole of my right foot.

I say, "Red is the color that grounds me to you," one last time as the color moves back to my tailbone. When I feel sufficiently grounded, I move the energy a few inches upward and say, "The Tiger's Orange grounds me to my creativity." I am picturing the orange of a tiger, while I am saying this. This energy swirls around until I feel that I have become connected to my own creativity.

I move the energy back to my tailbone and then up to a point below my solar plexus. I visualize the sun in the sky and say, "The sun's yellow grounds me to my power." I stay with this sensation until I feel grounded in my own sense of power.

Next, I move the energy up my spine until it connects to my heart, and I say, "Green is the color that connects me to my love to be shared." I then move it up my spine until it is connected to my throat, and I say, "Blue is the color that connects me to my voice to be heard." I am concentrating this entire time and visualizing the energy and the colors.

I then move the energy up until it connects to what yogis refer to as the "third eye."

This is a spot between and slightly above my eyebrows. I say, "Indigo is the color that connects me to my innate wisdom to be shared."

The final chakra is reached by moving the energy to the crown of my head and saying, "White is the color that connects me to the light of ascension." Once I have completed the chakra rituals,

I return my attention to the third eye and reach out to what yogis call the "spiritual eye."

I say, "Indigo and White seek the spiritual eye." I then concentrate on making this connection. When I can visualize the spiritual eye, my final ritual is complete. This is not always easy. But if I persevere, I can do it. I stick with it even when I just want to throw in the towel and start my day.

I need to do these three sets of rituals every day.

The rewards are immense. I can transform myself from a grumpy sleepyhead into a spiritually connected and vibrant being every single day.

I cannot allow myself to take a day off. I am the type of addict who will find it easy to take two days off if I allow myself one. If I take two days off, I might go on vacation from doing the work and stop doing it entirely. I know this about myself. I comfort myself by saying, "I don't have to do this forever, just every day."

After these spiritual rituals have been completed, I feel connected to all life forms around me. Crows have adopted me, by way of example; I have become their friend. I can connect to people in ways that would've struck me as ludicrous before. There is no manual for how to do this. It was a feeling-out process for me.

When you are in the present moment you can avoid being weighed down by the future. These are just the tools and techniques I have developed for my own use to help me reach that goal. They should serve only as examples of what might work for you. They were not taught to me. I did not read them in a book. They developed over time through a process of trial and error.

I discarded what didn't work and kept that which did. I used my inner resonance as a guide in making these determinations. Getting in touch with this inner resonance meant getting in touch with a source of wisdom above and beyond my own.

Just as Jung described a collective unconscious that has found its way into mainstream thinking, I believe we have a collective super-consciousness. All the true wisdom that has been found over the years has been passed down to us all.

When we tap into this collective super-consciousness, we can access the wisdom that is beyond our grasp as individuals. Some call this divine wisdom. I just know that it comes from somewhere beyond me.

It allows me to be connected to the saints, gurus, yogis, and mystics of the past.

Just as though they were with me in the present.

Who knows? Maybe they are.

These connections bring with them a whole new set of challenges. But that is another story entirely.

Epilogue

AA HAS HELPED A vast number of people. It has also failed to help many others. With its retention rate so low, how do many people find the help that they need?

There are numerous recovery programs. The addict needs to find the one that works best for them. It does not have to be the perfect program. It just must be the one that fits best for them.

Everyone's story will be different and this has been my story of how I found what worked for me.

It is best to focus on the similarities in our stories rather than the differences. It is rare that anyone can do it alone. When you find a program that best meets your needs, you will find a community.

It may be the first community where some of us feel like we truly belong, the community helping in ways which never seemed possible. Finding a community was an important part of my recovery.

If this book accomplishes only one thing, it will be to retrain the medical professionals and therapists that routinely refer their patients or clients to only a twelve-step program. If my thoughts raise their awareness of other programs available, it will have served its purpose.

There are many paths to recovery. The task is to find the one that works for you.

About the Author

James Eade was born in New Haven, Connecticut, in 1957. He graduated from the University of Massachusetts, Amherst in 1978. He got his Master's Degree from the University of San Francisco in 1991. He was an IT professional for AT&T and Charles Schwab. His lifelong association with chess began in 1972 when Bobby Fischer won the World Championship.

He played his first official tournament game that year and was awarded the title of Chess Master in 1981 by the national governing organization and in 1993 by the international governing organization. He wrote several books on chess, including the bestselling *Chess for Dummies*, and became active in chess governance in the early 1990s.

He is a past president of the Northern California Chess Association, the Chess Journalists of America, the United States Chess Trust, and his own foundation, the Eade Foundation, which he established in 2019 shortly after the death of his father, Arthur W. Eade, who taught him the game.

He was recognized as Chess Educator of the Year in 2016 by the University of Texas at Dallas, for his Outstanding Career Service by the US Chess Federation in 2018, and by Marquis Who's Who in 2022 for lifetime achievement. His foundation has helped build communities through chess on four continents.

Throughout his life, James battled with addiction to drugs and alcohol. This is the story of how he became free from the tyranny of addiction.

IF YOU'RE A FAN OF THIS BOOK, WILL YOU HELP ME SPREAD THE WORD?

- There are several ways you can help me get the word out about the message of this book...
- Post a 5-Star review on Amazon.
- Write about the book on your Facebook, Twitter, Instagram, LinkedIn – any social media you regularly use!
- If you blog, consider referencing the book, or publishing an excerpt from the book with a link back to my website. You have my permission to do this as long as you provide proper credit and backlinks.
- Recommend the book to friends – word-of-mouth is still the most effective form of advertising.
- Purchase additional copies to give away as gifts.

Email me at

jimeade@comcast.net

**Learn more about how the wisdom of
yoga can help anyone recover from addiction.**

A combination of lectures, group discussion,
gentle yoga postures,
and silent reflection/meditation.

Interested?

Email
vivekadevi@anandapaloalto.org